humility

Strength for Life

*Down, but Not Out: How to Get Up When Life Knocks
You Down*

Humility: The Forgotten Virtue

humility

the forgotten virtue

WAYNE A. MACK

with JOSHUA MACK

P&R
PUBLISHING
P.O. BOX 817 • PHILLIPSBURG • NEW JERSEY 08865-0817

Unless otherwise indicated, Scripture quotations are from the *NEW AMERICAN STANDARD BIBLE*®. © Copyright 1960, 1962, 1963, 1968, 1971, 1972, 1973, 1975, 1977, 1995 by The Lockman Foundation. Used by permission. (www.Lockman.org)

Italics within Scripture quotations indicate emphasis added.

Page design by Kirk DouPonce, Dog Eared Design
Typesetting by Lakeside Design Plus

Printed in the United States of America

Library of Congress Cataloging-in-Publication Data

Mack, Wayne A.
    Humility—the forgotten virtue / Wayne A. Mack with Joshua Mack.
      p. cm. — (Strength for life)
    Includes bibliographical references and index.
    ISBN-13: 978-0-87552-639-3
    ISBN-10: 0-8755-639-X
    1. Humility—Religious aspects—Christianity. 2. Humility—
Biblical teaching. I. Mack, Joshua. II. Title.

BV4647.H8M33 2005
241'.4—dc22

                                                   2005047678

Dedicated to the family of God that form
the congregation at
Grace Fellowship Church of the Lehigh Valley;

To Dan and Yvonne Retzlaf
and to my wife Carol,
who manifest a large amount of the virtue
described in this book.

CONTENTS

FOREWORD

Finally—a book that exposes the truth about pride and promotes what Cotton Mather called "the contrary grace,"[1] namely, humility. How sorely this book is needed in a day when scores of people are drowning in their own forms of unbiblical self-esteem!

Wayne Mack defines pride and humility biblically. He shows us in a multitude of ways that God hates pride (Prov. 6:16–17). He hates the proud with His heart, curses them with His mouth, and punishes them with His hand (Ps. 119:21; Isa. 2:12; 23:9). Pride was God's first enemy. It was the first sin in paradise and is the last we will shed in death. "Pride is the shirt of the soul, put on first and put off last," wrote George Swinnock.[2]

Mack shows us that as a sin, pride is unique. Most sins turn us away from God, but pride is a direct attack upon God. It lifts our hearts above Him and against Him. Pride seeks to dethrone God and enthrone itself.

Pride also seeks to dethrone my neighbor, we are told. It always puts self-idolatry above neighbor-service. At root, pride breaks both tables of the law and all Ten Commandments.

Pride is complex. "It takes many forms and shapes and encompasses the heart like the layers of an onion—when you pull off one layer, there is another underneath," wrote Jonathan Edwards.[3]

Pride feeds off nearly anything: a fair measure of ability and wisdom, a single compliment, a season of remarkable prosperity, or a small accomplishment. "It is hard starving this sin, as there is nothing almost but it can live upon," wrote Richard Mayo.[4]

Our forefathers did not consider themselves immune to this sin. "I know I am proud; and yet I do not know the half of that pride," wrote Robert Murray M'Cheyne.[5] Twenty years after his conversion, Jonathan Edwards groaned about the "bottomless, infinite depths of pride" left in his heart. And Martin Luther said, "I am more afraid of pope 'self' than of the pope in Rome and all his cardinals."[6]

A godly person fights against pride, whereas a worldly person feeds pride. "Men frequently admire me, and I am pleased," said Henry Martyn, adding, "but I abhor the pleasure I feel."[7] Cotton Mather confessed that when pride filled him with bitterness and confusion before the Lord, "I endeavoured to take a view of my pride as the very image of the Devil, contrary to the image and grace of Christ; as an offense against God, and grieving of His Spirit; as the most unreasonable folly and madness for one who had nothing singularly excellent and who had a nature so corrupt."[8] Thomas Shepard also fought pride. In his diary entry for November 10, 1642, Shepard wrote, "I kept a private fast for light to see the full glory of the Gospel . . . and for the conquest of all my remaining pride of heart."[9]

How do we fight against pride? Do we understand how deeply rooted it is in us? Do we ever remonstrate ourselves like the Puritan Richard Mayo: "Should that man be proud that has sinned as thou hast sinned, and lived as thou hast lived, and wasted so much time, and abused so much mercy, and omitted so many duties, and neglected so great means?—that hath so grieved the Spirit of God, so violated the law of God, so dishonoured the name of God? Should that man be proud, who hath such a heart as thou hast?"[10]

If we would kill worldly pride and live in godly humility, let us follow Mack's advice to look at our Savior, whose life, Calvin said, "was naught but a series of sufferings." Nowhere is humility so cultivated than at Gethsemane and Calvary. Confess with Joseph Hall:

> Thy garden is the place,
> Where pride cannot intrude;
> For should it dare to enter there,
> T'would soon be drowned in blood.

And sing with Isaac Watts:

> When I survey the wondrous cross
> On which the Prince of glory died,
> My richest gain I count but loss,
> And pour contempt on all my pride.

Here are some other ways to help you subdue pride and cultivate humility:

- Seek a deeper knowledge of God, His attributes, and His glory. Job and Isaiah teach us that nothing is so humbling as knowing God (Job 42; Isa. 6).
- Meditate much on the solemnity of death, the certainty of Judgment Day, and the vastness of eternity.
- View each day as an opportunity to forget yourself and serve others. The act of service is innately humbling.
- Read the biographies of great saints, such as George Whitefield's *Journals, The Life of David Brainerd,* and Charles Spurgeon's *Early Years.* As Dr. Martyn Lloyd-Jones says, "If that does not bring you to earth, then I pronounce that you are . . . beyond hope."[11]
- Remember daily that "pride goeth before destruction, and an haughty spirit before a fall" (Prov. 16:18 KJV). Pray daily for humility.
- Read this book. Answer the study questions. Then read the book again. If you take it seriously, and the Spirit blesses it to your heart, you will grow spiritually. The essence of that growth will be John the Baptist's confession, which I believe is the essence of all genuine sanctification: "He [Christ] must increase, but I must decrease" (John 3:30).

—Joel R. Beeke

PREFACE

Charles Spurgeon said, "That demon of pride was born with us, and it will not die one hour before us. It is so woven into the very warp and woof of our nature, that till we are wrapped in our winding-sheets we shall never hear the last of it."[1] In essence, pride is the first sin to rear its head when we're born and the last to go when we die. Pride is a serious problem for us throughout our lives. In similar fashion, C. S. Lewis evidences his conviction about the seriousness of pride in this way. In his book *Mere Christianity*, Lewis asserts that pride is "the essential vice, the utmost evil," and that it is the "one vice of which no man in the world is free, and of which hardly any people . . . ever imagine they are guilty themselves."[2] Chrysostom, an early church leader, joined his voice to these perspectives when he said that pride is the mother of all evils.[3]

No one who knows the Bible and is a careful observer of human beings will dispute that pride is and always has been a gigantic problem in the world. Nor can anyone dispute that pride causes serious problems and that its counterpart, humility, is a valuable, yet rare, quality in human beings and their relationships. Pride is endemic and natural for all of us who live this side of Genesis 3. True humility is exceptional and unnatural for all of us who live this side of heaven.

This book was written in an attempt to understand pride and humility from a biblical perspective and to help us diminish the destructive pride factor and to increase the true humility factor in our lives. To do this, I have used a four-*D* approach. First, based on the conviction that we can't put something off or put something on unless we know what that something is, I begin this book by giving a biblical *definition* of what pride and humility are. Then I discuss how pride and humility *display* themselves. And finally, I explain how true humility can be *developed* and destructive pride can be *diminished* in our lives.

God, says the Scripture, is opposed to proud people and gracious to humble people (James 4:6; 1 Peter 5:5). For this reason and many more that are explained in this book, every Christian should be vitally concerned about the subject under consideration. In His Word, we are told that the Lord Jesus Christ, the very Son of God manifest in the flesh, was meek and lowly (Matt. 11:28–30; Phil. 2:5–8). In His Word, God has told us that He wants all of us who have been redeemed through the obedience and sacrifice of Christ to be conformed to His image (Rom. 8:29–30; Phil. 2:5). Part of being conformed to His image involves putting off pride and putting on humility. My prayer is that God will use the material found in this volume to accomplish His purpose of our becoming more like the meek and lowly Jesus, our great Redeemer and

Lord and Example. Please join with me in praying that God will use this book to further that purpose in your life and mine.

Many people have been involved in helping me bring this book to fruition. To them I owe a great debt of gratitude. Without their help, in the midst of a very busy schedule, this book would have never come into existence. As you read the book, you may find some mistakes, in that I haven't been inspired as the biblical writers were. You may also find that the style is not as scintillating as you might like. Please blame me for any negative thing about the book and give these dear people who helped me the credit for any of the positives. They have been of immense help in birthing this book.

Who are these people? In a sense, all the people of Grace Fellowship Church of the Lehigh Valley of Pennsylvania helped me to develop this book, in that the material presented in it was first presented to them in our training-hour classes. They listened and responded to the material; it is my hope that they grew in their Christian lives through it.

More specifically, Janet Dudek, who has helped me with several other books, was initially responsible for typing and editing the contents. She spent many hours at this task. Her skill in helping me condense and phrase the material and her dedication, hard work, and support were invaluable. Her husband, Jeff, an English teacher, looked over her shoulder (and, figuratively speaking, mine as well) and gave valuable critique of grammar and style. Dr. Joel Beeke, a gifted and busy pastor, seminar professor, and church leader, graciously agreed to write a foreword to the book. As you read it, I think you'll realize why I'm so thankful to him for taking the time to read the book and write the foreword. His words set a wonderful tone for the rest of the book.

My wife, Carol, did her usual thing—reading the manuscripts and making comments on better ways of stating the information.

As you read this book, you will also become aware of other people who gave me an immense amount of help in writing it. Thomas Watson, John Bunyan, Jonathan Edwards, and Charles Spurgeon have provided valuable insights on the subject being discussed in this book through their written materials. Because you will find quotes from these men throughout this book, I would be remiss not to acknowledge the assistance I have received from them.

Thanks to all these people, but especially thanks to God for His goodness and for His giving me something to write about. I pray that this book will be mightily used to bring glory to our triune God and great blessing to His people, for whom Christ died and rose again.

1

THE IMPORTANCE OF HUMILITY

In John Bunyan's insightful book *The Pilgrim's Progress*, an allegory is used to teach great truth about the Christian faith and life. Bunyan's main character is called Christian, and this person goes on a long journey, beginning with salvation and ending in glory. At one point in the story, Christian is preparing to leave the Palace Beautiful, which represents the church, and descend into the valley of humiliation. Several friends will accompany him.

> Now it seemed to him that it was time to go and they agreed.
> "But first," they said, "let us take you to the Armory again."
> When they got there, they equipped Christian from head to foot with all he would need in case he

were attacked on the way. He then walked with his friends to the gate and there he asked Watchful, the gatekeeper, if he had seen any pilgrims pass by.

"Yes," Watchful answered.

"Please tell me, was it someone you knew?" asked Christian.

"I asked his name," said Watchful, "and he told me it was Faithful."

"Oh I know him," said Christian. "He is from my home town—a close neighbor. How far ahead do you think he is?"

"By this time, he should be down the hill."

"Well, kind sir, may the Lord be with you and bless you greatly for all the kindness you have shown me."

As he resumed his journey, Discretion, Piety, Charity and Prudence decided to accompany him to the foot of the hill. So they went out together reviewing some of their previous conversations until they reached the place where the hill began to descend.

Then Christian said, "It was difficult coming up the hill, and as far as I can see, going down looks treacherous."

"Yes, it is," said Prudence. "It is a very difficult thing for a man to go down into the valley of humiliation and not slip on the way. That is why we want to accompany you down the hill." So he began to make his way down very carefully, but even then he lost his footing once or twice.

Then I saw in my dream that when they reached the bottom of the Hill, Christian's dear companions gave him a Loaf of Bread, a Bottle of Wine, and a Cluster of Raisins. And he went on his way.[1]

What did Bunyan intend by the "valley of humiliation"? Why would Christian, fresh from becoming a member of the church, need to go there? Why do all believers find themselves, from time to time, in this same valley? What do we need to learn there? For the next several chapters, we are going to answer these and many other questions relating to the subject of humility.

THE VALLEY OF HUMILIATION: BIBLICAL EXAMPLES

The valley of humiliation represents the humbling experiences that God brings into our lives to destroy the sin of pride and to help us develop godly humility. Humbling experiences are common for us as believers today, just as they have been for all other believers throughout history. The Bible records many of these experiences for us.

In Genesis 12 we read about Abraham's humiliation before Pharaoh when he lied about Sarah's being his wife. For some time, Abraham enjoyed the hospitality of Pharaoh during a time of famine in the region, but Abraham and his household were eventually thrown out of the land because of this deception.

Joseph endured many years of humiliation before God placed him in the high position of prime minister of Egypt. First, he was abused and sold into slavery by his own brothers

(Gen. 37). Later, he was falsely accused of taking advantage of Potiphar's wife and spent two years in prison (Gen. 39–40).

Moses, who led the Israelites out of Egypt, was misunderstood and humiliated by his own brother and sister when they accused him of not sharing leadership over the people (Num. 12). In fact, God had commanded Moses to be their sole leader at that time. And many times during their exodus and wandering through the wilderness, the people of Israel complained against Moses even though they were responsible for their own situation. In fact, the Israelites spent forty years in the valley of humiliation—the wilderness—as God prepared them for the promised land. Other Old Testament examples include Eli, David, Elijah, Jeremiah, Hosea, and many others.

In the New Testament, we read about the humiliation of the apostles, including Peter, John, and Paul. These men spent time in prison for false crimes, they were beaten and threatened, and some were eventually killed. In 2 Corinthians, Paul wrote about a particular trial of humiliation that he dealt with constantly: "Because of the surpassing greatness of the revelations, for this reason, to keep me from exalting myself, there was given me a thorn in the flesh, a messenger of Satan to torment me—to keep me from exalting myself!" (12:7). If such a man as Paul needed to learn humility, we may be sure that we do as well.

THE IMPORTANCE OF HUMILITY IN THE CHRISTIAN LIFE

On one occasion, someone approached Augustine and asked, "What is the most important quality in the Christian life?" Augustine responded, "Humility." The person then asked, "What is the second most important quality in the Christian life?" Again Augustine responded, "Humility." This same person asked a third time, "What is the third most important quality in the Christian life?" Augustine repeated, "Humility."

We may judge from this exchange that Augustine deemed humility to be a tremendously important part of the Christian life. Whether or not the quality of humility—or any other particular Christian life quality—should be ranked higher than any other may be debated, but God's Word makes it very clear that humility is extremely important for believers.

We know this for several reasons. First, *we know that humility is tremendously important because the Bible frequently commands us to be humble.* First Peter 5:5–6 admonishes "all of you [to] *clothe yourselves* with humility toward one another. . . . Therefore *humble yourselves* under the mighty hand of God, that He may exalt you at the proper time." Notice that this is written as a command, not a suggestion. To fail to humble oneself is to disobey God, and such disobedience is sin.

In Ephesians 4:1–2, the apostle Paul wrote, "Therefore I, the prisoner of the Lord, implore you to walk in a manner worthy of the calling with which you have been called, with all humility and gentleness. . . ." Again, we are commanded in James 4:10, "Humble yourselves in the presence of the Lord, and He will exalt you."

Our Lord Jesus Christ called us to humility in Matthew 23:10–12: "Do not be called leaders; for One is your Leader, that is, Christ. But the greatest among you shall be your servant. Whoever exalts himself shall be humbled; and whoever humbles himself shall be exalted." The fact that these and many other Scriptures command us to be humble indicates that humility is extremely important.

Second, *we know that humility is very important because the Bible frequently warns us to rid ourselves of pride and warns us of its serious consequences.* Proverbs 16:5 says, "Everyone who is proud in heart is an abomination to the LORD; assuredly, he will not be unpunished." According to Proverbs 18:12, "Before destruction the heart of man is haughty. . . ." Isaiah 5:15 declares, "So the common man will be humbled and the man of importance abased, the eyes of the proud also will be abased." Pride is a serious sin that God does not tolerate, and the Bible makes it very clear that pride has no place in the Christian life.

Third, *we know that humility is important because God promises to bless those who are humble in heart.* James 4:6 says, "God is opposed to the proud, but gives grace to the humble." Proverbs 15:33 teaches, "The fear of the LORD is the instruction for wisdom, and before honor comes humility." Proverbs 22:4 promises, "The reward of humility and the fear of the LORD are riches, honor, and life." And Isaiah contains a wonderful promise to humble people: "For thus says the high and exalted One who lives forever, whose name is Holy, 'I dwell on a high and holy place, and also with the contrite and lowly of spirit in order to revive the spirit of the lowly and to revive the heart of the contrite' " (Isa. 57:15).

A common adage proclaims: "God helps those who help themselves." In fact, nothing could be more diametrically opposed to the truth of the Word of God than that. Scripture teaches that God helps those who come to Him for help and who depend on Him alone for all that they need. Indeed, God delights in blessing the humble person.

Jesus taught this principle to His disciples on several occasions. At the beginning of the Sermon on the Mount, He said, "Blessed are the poor in spirit, for theirs is the kingdom of heaven" (Matt. 5:3). Later, when the disciples were arguing about which of them was the greatest, Jesus called a child over to Himself and said to them, "Whoever then humbles himself as this child, he is the greatest in the kingdom of heaven" (Matt. 18:4).

While a humble person may not experience blessing as this world defines blessing, God promises that the humble in heart will know *His* blessing. As believers, we know that this blessing is of far greater worth than anything and everything in this physical world. Humility is indeed a very important quality in the Christian life.

GOD'S PURPOSE IN THE VALLEY OF HUMILIATION

Why does God take His people into the valley of humiliation? First, the fact that Scripture teaches the tremendous importance of humility implies that God highly values humility and despises pride. The many promises that God makes in the Scripture to bless those who are humble and to destroy those who are proud confirm this.

Second, God takes believers into the valley of humiliation because we are so prone to pride and so averse to humility. Humility is not something that we are born with. We are born proud, and because of our sinful hearts, we do not naturally seek after God. Psalm 10:4 teaches, "The wicked, in the haughtiness of his countenance, does not seek Him. All his thoughts are, 'There is no God.' " Apart from the grace of God in our lives, we all naturally tend to ignore God and exalt ourselves.

Thankfully, we have a God who is too merciful and gracious to let us go on in our pride. He knows that we all struggle with this sin to some degree—some of us more than others—and He wants to deliver us from our sinful pride. We all desperately need to learn how to turn away from pride and how to embrace humility, and so He uses the trials of the valley of humiliation to do this.

Third, God allows us to undergo humbling circumstances because He wants to test and increase our faith. First Peter 1:6–7 says, "In this you greatly rejoice, even though now for a little while, if necessary, you have been distressed by various trials, so that the proof of your faith . . . may be found to result in praise and glory and honor at the revelation of Jesus Christ." Our faith is made stronger only as it is exercised and tested.

Fourth, God leads us into the valley of humiliation because He wants to use the trials in our lives to produce in us a quality of endurance so that we may become "perfect and complete, lacking in nothing" (James 1:2–4). And finally, according to 2 Corinthians 12:7–10, God brings humiliating circumstances into our lives because they teach us to depend more on His all-sufficient grace. As Paul noted, "Therefore I am well content with weaknesses . . . for Christ's sake; for when I am weak, then I am strong."

As painful and discouraging as the valley of humiliation may be, if we set our minds on the good that God is doing there and understand His purposes, we can maintain our joy.

This is what James was talking about when he wrote, "*Consider it all joy*, my brethren, when you encounter various trials, knowing that the testing of your faith produces endurance" ✳ (James 1:2–3). Ultimately, as we grow in humility, we are becoming more and more like our Lord Jesus Christ, and that is a great privilege!

AN IMPORTANT CAUTION

In the rest of this chapter and for the next several chapters on this subject, we will consider three important aspects of humility: its definition, its display, and its development. Before we continue, however, it is of utmost importance that we remind ourselves to be careful not to make this study of pride and humility merely a matter of head knowledge. Rather, we must constantly and honestly examine ourselves for the presence of pride in our hearts so that we can repent of it. At the same time, we should be looking for ways to put humility into practice every day. Above all, we should be seeking the Lord's help in prayer for the desire and determination to diligently work on this area of our Christian life.

HUMILITY DEFINED

In order to define humility, we will start by looking at the definition of humility's opposite: pride. What is pride? Pride consists in attributing to ourselves and demanding for ourselves the honor, privileges, prerogatives, rights, and power that are due to God alone. Thus, it is the very root and essence of sin because pride, at its core, is idolatry of self. A proud person has put himself or herself in God's place.

Humility, then, consists in an attitude wherein we recognize our own insignificance and unworthiness before God and attribute to Him the supreme honor, praise, prerogatives, rights, privileges, worship, devotion, authority, submission, and obedience that He alone deserves. It also involves a natural, habitual tendency to think and behave in a manner that appropriately expresses this attitude. In other words, the attitude of humility is always seen in humble actions. It means having a servant's mind-set and always putting self last.

Now that we have generally defined humility, let us consider each aspect of this definition so that we can more fully understand this important quality. The more we understand in detail what true humility is, the better we will understand our own deficiency and great need of more of it in our lives.

First, *a truly humble person has an abiding sense of his natural insignificance, as compared to God.* Abraham exhibited this attitude when he said, " 'Now behold, I have ventured to speak to the Lord, although I am but dust and ashes' " (Gen. 18:27). Abraham was deeply aware of the incredible insignificance of his knowledge and understanding compared to the wisdom of God. Job also showed this aspect of humility when, after being thoroughly tested by God, he said, " 'Behold, I am insignificant; what can I reply to You? I lay my hand on my mouth' " (Job 40:4). Job finally came to the place of recognizing God's infinite natural superiority to man.

Humble people have a great sense of their ignorance, their weakness, and their unimportance. They know that if "the nations are like a drop from a bucket" in God's eyes (Isa.

40:15), then they are far, far less than that. They recognize the insufficiency of their own power. They understand that only God is omniscient, omnipresent, omnipotent, all-wise, full of grace and truth and righteousness. They realize that they are totally dependent on God for everything: wisdom, health, safety, and even the ability to obey. In fact, it is only by God's grace that we can even do anything that pleases Him.

Still further, humble people are deeply aware of their lack of greatness and lack of right to exercise authority over anyone. On the other hand, they are acutely aware of God's greatness and God's supreme right to rule over all. This means that truly humble people put themselves entirely under God's authority. Whatever God says to do or not do, they obey completely and without question because they recognize the Creator–creature distinction. God is the Creator, and we are His creatures.

Second, *a truly humble person has an abiding sense of his moral insignificance and sinfulness, as compared to God.* Isaiah demonstrated this sense when he said, " 'Woe is me, for I am ruined! Because I am a man of unclean lips, and I live among a people of unclean lips' " (Isa. 6:5). The publican, in Luke 18:13, showed this aspect of humility as well when he stood at a distance from the altar, refused to look up to heaven, beat his chest, and said, " 'God, be merciful to me, the sinner!' "

To put it another way, a truly humble person has an accurate sense of his unworthiness before God. In Genesis 32:10, Jacob expressed this humility of spirit when he said, " 'I am unworthy of all the lovingkindness and of all the faithfulness which You have shown to Your servant. . . .' " David also acknowledged his unworthiness when he asked, " 'Who am

I, O Lord GOD, and what is my house, that You have brought me this far?' " (2 Sam. 7:18).

Indeed, truly humble people read a passage such as Romans 3:10–18 and think to themselves, "This is me! This is *my heart* that is being described":

> As it is written,
> "There is none righteous, not even one;
> There is none who understands,
> There is none who seeks for God;
> All have turned aside, together they have become
>   useless;
> There is none who does good,
> There is not even one."
> "Their throat is an open grave,
> With their tongues they keep deceiving,"
> "The poison of asps is under their lips";
> "Whose mouth is full of cursing and bitterness";
> "Their feet are swift to shed blood,
> Destruction and misery are in their paths,
> And the path of peace they have not known."
> "There is no fear of God before their eyes."

Third, *a person who is truly humble has a theocentric mind-set.* A person who thinks theocentrically puts God at the center of everything. God is his Master. This is in contrast to the proud person, who has an *anthropocentric* mind-set, in which man is at the center of everything. To be more exact, *self* is at the center of everything in the mind of the proud person. He is his own master, and everyone and everything else exists to please him and to serve his needs. As a result, he takes the throne in his own heart and, in reality, worships himself. Not only that, but he demands that everyone else worship him as well.

The humble person, on the other hand, has a servant's mind-set. He desires to worship, love, and serve God at all times, and he demonstrates this mind-set daily by loving and serving other people. He would much rather deny himself than exalt himself or be exalted by others. He has the mind of Christ, who said that " 'the Son of Man did not come to be served, but to serve, and to give His life a ransom for many' " (Matt. 20:28).

Fourth, *a person who is truly humble attributes to God supreme honor, praise, rights, and privileges.* God alone is worshiped and exalted, as Jesus said in Matthew 4:10: " 'For it is written, "You shall worship the LORD your God, and serve Him only." ' " A humble person is devoted to God in a way that he is devoted to no one else in his life. He acknowledges God as his supreme authority in all matters of life. What God says is what he does.

The humble man also recognizes that everything good that he has comes from the hand of God. He knows that God is the source of all things, the means of all things, and the goal of all things. He says with Paul, "For from Him and through Him and to Him are all things. To Him be the glory forever. Amen" (Rom. 11:36). He realizes that it is his great privilege to live his life for the glory of God in everything that he does because He alone is worthy.

PERSONAL EVALUATION

If we truly desire to grow in this quality of humility, we must be willing to take the time to honestly examine and evaluate ourselves in terms of this definition. Is our heart overwhelmed by the truth of our natural insignificance before the Almighty God? Are we painfully aware of our sinfulness and unworthiness before a Holy God? Is God the constant center around which our thoughts, desires, words, and actions revolve? Do we give Him alone our worship, praise, devotion, and obedience?

An honest appraisal of our hearts will no doubt reveal that we fall far short in all of these ways. None of us is truly humble as we ought to be and truly void of pride. Because I agree that pride is the first sin to rear its head when we're born and the last to go when we die, and because humility is such an important, but forgotten and neglected virtue, I encourage you to seriously and expectantly devour and apply the material in this book. In *The Pilgrim's Progress*, John Bunyan was on target biblically when he indicated that the valley of humiliation is a valley that every Christian will encounter and needs to encounter as he journeys through the wilderness of this world toward heaven. Praise God that He loves us so much that He is willing to humiliate us in order to rid us of our awful pride!

APPLICATION / DISCUSSION EXERCISES

1. What biblical reasons are there for believing that humility is an important aspect of the Christian life?

2. How is humility defined in this chapter?

3. How does this chapter describe a truly humble person?

4. Are you a person who has a self-centered outlook on life? How frequently do you think of yourself as a person whom others should serve, respect, and please?

[ ] often   [ ] sometimes   [ ] seldom   [ ] never [ ]

5. When other people do not respect or please you, how frequently do you criticize, judge, or punish them for not treating you as you "deserve" to be treated?

[ ] often   [ ] sometimes   [ ] seldom   [ ] never [ ]

6. How frequently do you have a God-centered outlook on life?

[ ] often   [ ] sometimes   [ ] seldom   [ ] never [ ]

7. How frequently do you think about how you can serve, please, and encourage other people?

[ ] often   [ ] sometimes   [ ] seldom   [ ] never [ ]

8. How frequently do you deny your desires, pleasures, or needs for the sake of others?

[ ] often   [ ] sometimes   [ ] seldom   [ ] never [ ]

9. List some illustrations of times when you have served, sought to please, and encouraged people without having any thought of getting anything in return.

2

HUMILITY
TOWARD GOD

In the Christian life, the way up is down. Jesus taught, "For everyone who exalts himself will be humbled, and he who humbles himself will be exalted" (Luke 14:11). In the introduction to this book, I introduced the "four *D*s"— the definition of pride and humility, the display of pride and humility, and the development of humility and the diminishing of pride—and looked specifically at the *definition* of humility. By implication, we also defined humility's opposite, pride.

In this chapter, we are going to consider the *display* of humility in order to answer the following question: How is humility manifested in terms of our attitudes and actions before God? In the next chapter, we will consider how humility manifests itself before other people.

✳ *The first way in which true humility manifests itself before God is by the free and sincere confession of one's insignificance and sinfulness.* David made this confession in Psalm 8:4: "What is man that You take thought of him, and the son of man that You care for him?" In other words, a humble person honestly marvels at the fact that the Creator of the universe—the High and Holy One, the Almighty God—cares for him or even takes note of him.

Paul showed this kind of humility when he wrote, "It is a trustworthy statement, deserving full acceptance, that Christ Jesus came into the world to save sinners, among whom I am foremost of all" (1 Tim. 1:15). Though most of us regard Paul as a great servant of the Lord, Paul was able to make this statement because he knew himself the best. Knowing his own heart, Paul could say that he was the greatest of sinners and that his salvation was nothing more than a testimony of God's amazing grace. "Yet for this reason I found mercy, so that in me as the foremost, Jesus Christ might demonstrate His perfect patience as an example for those who would believe in Him for eternal life" (1 Tim. 1:16).

Not only that, but the only thing that Paul would ever brag about was the cross of Christ: "But may it never be that I would boast, except in the cross of our Lord Jesus Christ, through which the world has been crucified to me, and I to the world" (Gal. 6:14). A truly humble person, like Paul, will always confess his unworthiness to receive anything from the hand of God.

This was the attitude of the Canaanite woman who came to Jesus in Matthew 15 and begged, "Have mercy on me, Lord,

Son of David; my daughter is cruelly demon-possessed" (15:22). After she said this, Jesus appeared to ignore her until His disciples insisted that He send her away. "But He answered and said, 'I was sent only to the lost sheep of the house of Israel.' But she came and began to bow down before Him, saying, 'Lord, help me!' And He answered and said, 'It is not good to take the children's bread and throw it to the dogs.' But she said, 'Yes, Lord; but even the dogs feed on the crumbs which fall from their masters' table' " (Matt. 15:24–27).

Jesus, in His wisdom and mercy, reminded this woman of her great unworthiness before Him. Most of us, having essentially been called a "dog" in public, would have angrily lashed back or immediately turned away. The remarkable thing is that this woman, instead of reacting with sinful pride, humbly admitted to Jesus and everyone else present that she was indeed unworthy and continued to beg for Jesus' mercy. What an example of true humility!

Additionally, truly humble people freely admit that anything they do that is good is really of God. They take no credit for anything worthwhile that is accomplished through them. Paul admitted as much in 2 Corinthians 3:5 when he wrote, "Not that we are adequate in ourselves to consider anything as coming from ourselves, but our adequacy is from God." He gave God all the credit for his ministry, saying in 1 Corinthians 3:6–7, "I planted, Apollos watered, but God was causing the growth. So then neither the one who plants nor the one who waters is anything, but God who causes the growth."

A second way that humility manifests itself before God is by a complete lack of trust in one's own heart and complete dependence on God for all things. A truly humble person will heartily agree with Jeremiah 17:9, which says, "The heart is more deceitful than all else and is desperately sick; who can understand it?" Knowing this, the person heeds the warning in Proverbs 28:26, "He who trusts in his own heart is a fool. . . ."

Truly humble people depend on God for all wisdom and instruction. In fact, they greatly distrust the opinions of their own hearts. Romans 3:4 says, "Rather, let God be found true, though every man be found a liar. . . ." Instead of setting their or others' opinions over the perspectives of an all-knowing, wise God, humble people admit that man is often wrong and that God is always right. Isaiah 2:22 reminds, "Stop regarding man, whose breath of life is in his nostrils; for why should he be esteemed?" A truly humble person never trusts in himself for anything.

God rebuked the Israelites time and time again for trusting in themselves rather than depending on Him. In Isaiah 9:8–12, we find this declaration from the Lord:

> The Lord sends a message against Jacob,
> And it falls on Israel.
> And all the people know it,
> That is, Ephraim and the inhabitants of Samaria,
> Asserting in pride and in arrogance of heart:
> "The bricks have fallen down,
> But we will rebuild with smooth stones;
> The sycamores have been cut down,
> But we will replace them with cedars."
> Therefore the LORD raises against them adversaries
>   from Rezin
> And spurs their enemies on,

The Arameans on the east and the Philistines on the
   west;
And they devour Israel with gaping jaws.
In spite of all this, His anger does not turn away
And His hand is still stretched out.

The children of Israel had confidence in their own
resources and strength to rebuild their cities. They boasted
that they could build bigger and better than what had been
before, but God saw their proud and self-sufficient hearts and
passed judgment on them. He sent other nations to destroy
them because they refused to admit their dependence on Him
for all things.

In our world, we often see man esteemed above all else,
especially people who are perceived to be the most powerful,
wealthiest, most intelligent, or most talented. Jeremiah 9:23
warns against the futility of this kind of thinking: "Thus says
the Lord, 'Let not a wise man boast of his wisdom, and let
not the mighty man boast of his might, let not a rich man
boast of his riches. . . .' " All of these things are merely gifts
from the Almighty God, whose power is infinite, who has all
the universe at His disposal, and whose wisdom and creativ-
ity are beyond our comprehension.

In reality, we have nothing to boast of other than this:
" 'but let him who boasts boast of this, that he understands
and knows Me, that I am the Lord who exercises lovingkindness, justice and righteousness on earth; for I delight
in these things,' declares the Lord" (Jer. 9:24). We, humble
creatures that are made of dust and whose lives are but a breath,
can know and understand the Almighty God—that is something to boast about! Notice, however, that making this boast

requires great humility because it requires us to admit—rightly so—that we are nothing.

As truly humble people, we need to depend on God completely—for all things at all times. I believe that is why God sometimes allows us to be let down by other people. When other people break their promises or let us down in some way, it causes us to turn to God and to remember that putting our trust in man is foolish. Consider the words of Jeremiah:

> Thus says the LORD,
> "Cursed is the man who trusts in mankind
> And makes flesh his strength,
> And whose heart turns away from the LORD.
> "For he will be like a bush in the desert
> And will not see when prosperity comes,
> But will live in stony wastes in the wilderness,
> A land of salt without inhabitant.
> "Blessed is the man who trusts in the LORD
> And whose trust is the LORD.
> "For he will be like a tree planted by the water,
> That extends its roots by a stream
> And will not fear when the heat comes;
> But its leaves will be green,
> And it will not be anxious in a year of drought
> Nor cease to yield fruit." (Jer. 17:5–8)

When we humbly place our trust in God alone, we will find that we are sustained and blessed by Him continuously. If, on the other hand, our trust is in people, we will often find ourselves left dry in difficult times. Only God's strength, His provision, His comfort, and His wisdom do not change. He is that stream which never, ever runs dry and which will sustain us at all times.

A third way that humility manifests itself before God is by totally renouncing any glory coming from our own good and by giving all glory to God for all things. Psalm 115:1 says, "Not to us, O Lord, not to us, but to Your name give glory because of Your lovingkindness, because of Your truth." In 1 Corinthians 4:7, Paul reminded his readers that everything they had came from God: "For who regards you as superior? What do you have that you did not receive? And if you did receive it, why do you boast as if you had not received it?"

If we are more talented than others, are we ultimately responsible for it? No. Are our parents responsible for it? No. God made us and endowed us with the gifts and abilities that we have. Our talents, our possessions, our intelligence, our personalities, our relationships, and everything else with which we have been blessed are from God. As Paul said, "But by the grace of God I am what I am . . ." (1 Cor. 15:10).

In the Old Testament, Job was a man greatly blessed by God in a material way. He had thousands of animals, many servants, ten children, and many other possessions. Scripture says that he was "the greatest of all the men of the east" (Job 1:3). And yet, when all of these things were taken away from Job, Job humbly acknowledged that everything he had was of the Lord. "He said, 'Naked I came from my mother's womb, and naked I shall return there. The Lord gave and the Lord has taken away. Blessed be the name of the Lord' " (Job 1:21).

The Israelites often struggled with giving God all the glory for what they had. For forty years of wandering in the wilderness, they depended on God daily for every provision, but God knew that their hearts were still proud. Before leading them into the promised land, a land of great resources, God warned them to not let pride cloud their memories and distort their thinking:

> "For the LORD your God is bringing you into a good land, . . . a land where you will eat food without scarcity, in which you will not lack anything. . . . When you have eaten and are satisfied, you shall bless the LORD your God for the good land which He has given you.
>
> "Beware that you do not forget the LORD your God by not keeping His commandments and His ordinances and His statutes which I am commanding you today; otherwise, when you have eaten and are satisfied, and have built good houses and lived in them, and when your herds and your flocks multiply, and your silver and gold multiply, and all that you have multiplies, then your heart will become proud and you will forget the LORD your God. . . . Otherwise, you may say in your heart, 'My power and the strength of my hand made me this wealth.' But you shall remember the LORD your God, for it is He who is giving you power to make wealth. . . ." (Deut. 8:7–18)

This was a warning to the Israelites and to us about the propensity human beings have to take credit for themselves for that which God really deserves the credit. How often do we take an undeserved amount of credit for good things that we have or that we have done? The answer must be: All too often. In a sermon titled "The Scales of Judgment" Charles

Spurgeon described how prone we are to do the very thing that God warns against in the Deuteronomy passage:

> How many have been destroyed by prosperity! The fumes of popularity have turned the brains of many a man. The adulation of multitudes has laid thousands low. . . . Many have I known who in a cottage seemed to fear God, but in a mansion have forgotten him. When their daily bread was earned with the sweat of their brow, then it was they served the Lord, and went up to his house with gladness. But their seeming religion all departed when their flocks and herds increased, and their gold and silver was multiplied. It is no easy thing to stand the trial of prosperity. . . . What the storms of affliction never could accomplish, the soft hand and the witchery of prosperity has been able to perform. . . . [Prosperity] has been the Delilah that has shorn the locks and taken away the strength of many a Samson. This rock has witnessed the most fatal wrecks.[1]

In still another sermon titled "The Fruitless Vine" Spurgeon spoke of this wicked and groundless propensity to exalt ourselves rather than God:

> O! strange mystery, that thou, who hast borrowed everything, should exalt thyself; that thou, who hast nothing of thine own, but hast still to draw upon grace, shouldst be proud; a poor dependent pensioner upon the bounty of thy Saviour, and yet proud; one

who hath a life which can only live by fresh streams of life from Jesus, and yet proud![2]

"Every good and perfect gift is from above, coming down from the Father of heavenly lights" (James 1:17). We have nothing that we have not received, yet we often act and think as though we produced and deserved the good things we possess or should get the credit for the good works we have done. Why do we do this? Because we are proud. And, the truth is that when we take glory to ourselves that belongs only to God, we are committing robbery. The truth is that we are also liars because nothing we have or have done that is good is of us. The truth is that we are idolaters because we are giving ourselves praise that belongs to God alone. A truly humble person gives God praise and thanks for everything that he has and everything he has done that is good.

A fourth way that humility manifests itself before God is by respecting, receiving, and responding to the Word of God. In Isaiah 66:2, God describes a humble person this way: " 'But to this one I will look, to him who is humble and contrite of spirit, *and who trembles at My word.*' " A person who trembles before the Word of God is a person who takes God's Word very seriously. He listens carefully when it is spoken and responds to it with great conviction and repentance when he is admonished by it, as Josiah, king of Judah, did:

> Then Hilkiah the high priest said to Shaphan the scribe, "I have found the book of the law in the house of the LORD." And Hilkiah gave the book to Shaphan who read it. Shaphan the scribe came to the king and brought back word to the king and said, . . . "Hilkiah

the priest has given me a book." And Shaphan read it in the presence of the king.

When the king heard the words of the book of the law, he tore his clothes. Then the king commanded Hilkiah the priest, . . . saying, "Go, inquire of the LORD for me and the people and all Judah concerning the words of this book that has been found, for great is the wrath of the LORD that burns against us, because our fathers have not listened to the words of this book, to do according to all that is written concerning us." (2 Kings 22:8–13)

Josiah demonstrated his humility before God by responding to His Word with great conviction. By tearing his clothes, he showed the shame and sorrow that he felt in his heart because of the many sins that he and his people had committed. Likewise, when the Holy Spirit uses the Word of God to convict us of sin, our humble response should be to tremble at His Word.

A fifth way that humility is manifested before God is by completely submitting to God's will even if His will is difficult. In other words, a truly humble person takes his orders from God no matter what. Psalm 119:128 says, "Therefore I esteem right all Your precepts concerning everything, I hate every false way." Likewise, a truly humble person will never question the truth of God's Word.

More than that, a person who takes his orders from God will never question God's right to ordain the events of his life. Abraham was an example of a humble person in this way. In Genesis 12:1, God commanded Abraham: " 'Go forth from your country, and from your relatives and from your father's house, to the land which I will show you.' " Abraham, not knowing where he was going, went at God's command.

Imagine for a moment how hard it would be to uproot your household and move away from friends, family, and familiarity to a place that you had never been. It is a difficult thing to move out in faith in such a circumstance, leaving nearly all earthly security behind, knowing only that God is leading the way. But that knowledge was enough for Abraham. He obeyed God and believed His promises: " 'And I will make you a great nation, and I will bless you, and make your name great; and so you shall be a blessing; and I will bless those who bless you, and the one who curses you I will curse. And in you all the families of the earth will be blessed.' So Abram went forth . . ." (12:2–4).

Shadrach, Meshach, and Abednego also demonstrated humility by taking a stand against the emperor of Babylon, Nebuchadnezzar. In Daniel 3 we read about how these three young men refused to fall down and worship a golden image, though they knew that the consequences for failing to do so were severe. Instead of bowing to the command of men, they bowed to the command of God, "You shall have no other gods before Me" (Ex. 20:3). They submitted to God's will despite what could very well have meant physical death.

Our Lord Jesus Christ demonstrated the highest degree of humility and submission to the will of God when He "humbled Himself by becoming obedient to the point of death, even death on a cross" (Phil. 2:8). True humility evidences itself in a willingness to submit oneself to God's will no matter how difficult it may be.

For example, my father-in-law, a lawyer, once had to help some clients deal with the estate of a deceased relative. His clients, who were the beneficiaries of the will, asked my father-in-law to do something illegal in order to avoid paying some of the estate taxes that were due. Because of what he believed about God's laws and the importance of honesty, my father-in-law refused to do what they asked. As a result of his obedience to God, he lost the business of some longtime clients.

Obeying God can lead to unpleasant and difficult circumstances, but if we desire to manifest truly humble spirits, we must do it because God is the authority in our lives and we are not. A humble person always submits to and never questions God's authority.

A sixth way that humility is manifested before God is by submitting oneself to the providences of God without complaint. Those who grumble and complain about the circumstances of their lives are manifesting a spirit of pride. A person who complains about his circumstances does so because he thinks he deserves better. A humble person, on the other hand, willingly accepts whatever God ordains. He says with Paul, "I have learned to be content in whatever circumstances I am" (Phil. 4:11).

Consider the words of this wonderful hymn about humility:

> Whate'er my God ordains is right: holy his will
> abideth;
> I will be still whate'er he doth, and follow where he
> guideth:
> He is my God; though dark my road, he holds me that
> I shall not fall: wherefore to him I leave it all.

Whate'er my God ordains is right: he never will
  deceive me;
He leads me by the proper path; I know he will not
  leave me:
I take, content, what he hath sent; his hand can turn
  my griefs away, and patiently I wait his day.

Whate'er my God ordains is right: though now this
  cup, in drinking,
May bitter seem to my faint heart, I take it, all
  unshrinking:
My God is true; each morn anew sweet comfort yet
  shall fill my heart, and pain and sorrow shall depart.

Whate'er my God ordains is right: here shall my stand
  be taken;
Though sorrow, need, or death be mine, yet am I not
  forsaken;
My Father's care is round me there; he holds me that
  I shall not fall: and so to him I leave it all.[3]

Our Lord Jesus Christ was a great example of every aspect of true humility, including this one about submitting oneself to the providences of God without complaint. Though God incarnate, Jesus was described as being "gentle and humble in heart" (Matt. 11:29). He preached the most important message of all time to the people of His day and did miracles in their midst, but many people rejected Him.

Though Jesus' ministry in some places was largely a failure by human standards, Jesus manifested His humility before God by saying, " 'I praise You, Father, Lord of heaven and earth, that You have hidden these things from the wise and intelligent and have revealed them to infants. Yes, Father, for this way was well-pleasing in Your sight. All things have been handed over to Me by My Father . . .' " (Matt. 11:25–27). Christ humbly accepted the providences of God the Father in His life on earth.

A seventh way that humility is manifested before God is by delighting in the worship and praise of God. A humble person says with David, "I was glad when they said to me, 'Let us go to the house of the LORD' " (Ps. 122:1). Humble people long for corporate worship and fellowship with God as the psalmist did in Psalm 42: "As the deer pants for the water brooks, so my soul pants for You, O God. My soul thirsts for God, for the living God; when shall I come and appear before God?" (Ps. 42:1–2).

We see a similar desire expressed in Psalm 84, which is titled *Longing for Temple Worship.* The psalmist writes:

> How lovely are Your dwelling places,
> O LORD of hosts!
> My soul longed and even yearned for the courts of the
>   LORD;
> My heart and my flesh sing for joy to the living God.
> The bird also has found a house, and the swallow a
>   nest for herself, where she may lay her young,
> Even Your altars, O LORD of hosts,
> My King and my God.
> How blessed are those who dwell in Your house!
> They are ever praising You. (Ps. 84:1–4)

Do we long to worship God together with His people so much that we envy the birds that make their nests in the rafters of our church buildings? That is the longing of a humble person who realizes the need for and privilege of worshiping God.

An eighth way in which humility is manifested before God is by continually seeking God in prayer. Hardly anything is more an evidence of pride than prayerlessness. In Psalm 10:4, the Scripture describes unsaved and proud people: "The wicked, in the haughtiness of his countenance, does not seek Him. All his thoughts are, 'There is no God.'" Proud people do not pray, but the Word of God clearly connects humility with prayer. In 2 Chronicles 7:14, God says, "My people who are called by My name humble themselves and pray and seek My face. . . ."

We know, of course, that Jesus was a truly humble person, and the Scripture testifies that He continually sought the Father's face in prayer. He often spent long periods of time in prayer in secluded places. If the Son of God needed to spend time in prayer, how much more do we!

The apostle Paul, an extremely humble man, also spent much time in prayer. Almost every letter to the churches begins with evidence of his prayers for the people of God. He admonished his readers to be in constant prayer, and he coveted their prayers for himself. In fact, Paul credited the prayers of God's people for the things that he had accomplished in ministry: "You also join[ed] in helping us through your prayers, so that thanks may be given by many persons on our behalf for the favor bestowed on us through the prayers of many" (2 Cor. 1:11). A truly humble person constantly comes to God in prayer.

A ninth way that humility is manifested before God is by considering it a privilege to serve Christ in any capacity—a privilege that we are not worthy of or deserving. A truly humble person gladly serves the Lord regardless of the job, whether leading or following, preaching or taking out the trash, receiving thanks or being completely unnoticed by anyone. Moses is an excellent example, though he had to learn this kind of humility the hard way.

Moses was raised in the courts of Egypt as an adopted son of the daughter of Pharaoh. He received the best education of the day and had all the treasures of Egypt at his disposal. Scripture tells us,

> Now it came about in those days, when Moses had grown up, that he went out to his brethren and looked on their hard labors; and he saw an Egyptian beating a Hebrew, one of his brethren. So he looked this way and that, and when he saw there was no one around, he struck down the Egyptian and hid him in the sand. He went out the next day, and behold, two Hebrews were fighting each other; and he said to the offender, "Why are you striking your companion?" But he said, "Who made you a prince or judge over us? Are you intending to kill me as you killed the Egyptian?" (Ex. 2:11–14)

In these instances when Moses took it upon himself to be a protector and deliverer, he failed miserably and nearly got himself killed in that when "Pharaoh heard of the matter, he tried to kill Moses. But Moses fled from the presence of Pharaoh and settled in the land of Midian, and he sat by a well" (Ex.

2:15). Because of his actions, Moses went from the treasures of Egypt that he enjoyed as the adopted son of Pharaoh's daughter to the land of Midian where he must have experienced very meager and ordinary provisions. For Moses, that must have been a very humbling experience.

We can see that Moses learned his lesson in the wilderness when we consider his response to God in Exodus 3. At that time, God appeared to him in a burning bush and commanded him to lead the Israelites out of Egypt. While a proud person might have eagerly accepted this great mission, the now-humble Moses refused to think himself worthy of such a task. He replied to God, " 'Who am I, that I should go to Pharaoh, and that I should bring the sons of Israel out of Egypt?' " (3:11).

Paul also recognized that serving Christ was a privilege of which he was not worthy. In 2 Corinthians 2:16, he wrote that "to the one [we are] an aroma from death to death, to the other an aroma from life to life. And who is adequate for these things?" Paul knew that his ministry was a failure at times because some people rejected his preaching. A proud person would find it very difficult to not become discouraged, thinking he deserved to be listened to.

Other people responded to Paul's message and welcomed it with gladness. They turned to Christ and their lives were changed. A proud person would feel responsible for such success and would glory in the impact of his ministry. Paul, however, was neither discouraged by failure nor triumphant in success. He demonstrated his humility when he acknowledged that at all times, he was unworthy of the privilege of serving Christ.

Truly humble people will serve Christ no matter what the job is. They are willing to wash the feet of others as much as they are willing to lead because they have a humble and godly perspective on their work. Consider this illustration: Three men were working on constructing a church building. Someone approached the men and asked, "What are you doing?" The first man replied, "I'm laying bricks." The second said, "I'm earning money to put food on the table." The third answered, "I'm building a place where people will worship God and help each other."

All three men were doing the same thing, but their attitude toward their work was very different. A humble person can wash the feet of others and truly enjoy his work because he is doing it all for the glory of God. A proud person may become discouraged and bored by menial tasks because he thinks he deserves to be doing something greater. In truth, however, whatever we are called to do in life is exactly what God wants us to do, and it is our privilege to do it for His glory.

Consider the example of Jeremiah, a prophet of the Lord in the Old Testament. God came to Jeremiah and told him that He was about to pronounce judgment on His people through Jeremiah. God commanded Jeremiah to strengthen himself and not be afraid of the people because, as He explained, Jeremiah was going to be an obstacle to the people and they would fight against him:

> "Now, gird up your loins and arise, and speak to them all which I command you. Do not be dismayed before them, or I will dismay you before them. Now behold, I have made you today as a fortified city and as a pil-

lar of iron and as walls of bronze against the whole land, to the kings of Judah, to its princes, to its priests and to the people of the land. They will fight against you, but they will not overcome you, for I am with you to deliver you," declares the LORD. (Jer. 1:17–19)

In essence, God told Jeremiah that He was sending him on an impossible mission. He was to call the people of God to repentance and admonish them for their disobedience, but they were going to reject him and his message.

What was Jeremiah's response? He humbly accepted his commission from the Lord and went. He preached to people who did not care about what he had to say and even persecuted him for his message. Truly humble people consider it a privilege to serve Christ in *any* capacity—a privilege of which they are unworthy.

Finally, a tenth way that humility is manifested before God is by being willing to acknowledge God's infinite wisdom and knowledge. Job, for a period of time during his testing, was not humble in this way. In Job 23:1–5, we read: "Then Job replied, 'Even today my complaint is rebellion; His hand is heavy despite my groaning. Oh that I knew where I might find Him, that I might come to His seat! I would present my case before Him and fill my mouth with arguments. I would learn the words which He would answer, and perceive what He would say to me.' " In other words, Job wanted some answers from God. He wanted to argue and reason with God and ask some questions about his situation. God allowed Job to go on like this for a while, asking questions and demanding answers. Then, in chapter 38, God answered Job

out of the whirlwind and said,

"Who is this that darkens counsel

By words without knowledge?

"Now gird up your loins like a man,

And I will ask you, and you instruct Me!

"Where were you when I laid the foundation of the
earth?

Tell Me, if you have understanding,

Who set its measurements?

Since you know.

Or who stretched the line on it?" (Job 38:1–5)

God questioned Job for some time, making it abundantly clear that Job was in no position to question the One who had created the universe. Just as God did not need the wisdom or counsel of any man when He put the universe in order, He does not need to explain Himself to any man or listen to any man's counsel.

When Job finally got the message, he was humbled to the core. He said to God, " 'Behold, I am insignificant; what can I reply to You? I lay my hand on my mouth' " (Job 40:4). Later, he added, " 'I have heard of You by the hearing of the ear; but now my eye sees You; therefore I retract, and I repent in dust and ashes' " (Job 42:5–6).

Job became the type of person who humbly acknowledged God's superior knowledge, but it required a great trial. Proud people demand answers, as Job did. Proud people refuse to trust in God's sovereignty unless they can make sense of it themselves. Proud people do not want to admit that there are many things that only God can answer.

God does not owe us an explanation for anything in our lives. Deuteronomy 29:29 teaches, " 'The secret things belong to the LORD our God, but the things revealed belong to us and to our sons forever, that we may observe all the words of this law.' " According to His great wisdom, God has told us exactly what He wants us to know, and He has chosen to keep many other things from us. If we desire to manifest true humility in our lives, we must be willing to acknowledge that God's wisdom and knowledge are infinitely superior to ours.

My wife's favorite hymn, written by William Cowper, wonderfully expresses this aspect of a truly humble person in this way:

> God moves in a mysterious way his wonders to perform;
> He plants his footsteps in the sea, and rides upon the storm.
> Deep in unfathomable mines of never-failing skill
> He treasures up his bright designs, and works his sovereign will.
> Ye fearful saints, fresh courage take; the clouds ye so much dread
> Are big with mercy, and shall break in blessings on your head.
> Judge not the Lord by feeble sense, but trust him for his grace;
> Behind a frowning providence He hides a smiling face.
> His purposes will ripen fast, unfolding ev'ry hour;
> The bud may have a bitter taste, but sweet will be the flow'r.
> Blind unbelief is sure to err, and scan his work in vain;
> God is his own interpreter, and he will make it plain.[4]

Only a truly humble person can sing this hymn with integrity; the convictions of a proud person would make it impossible for him to honestly sing it. In pride, this man demands that God explain the mysteries of His providence and is upset with God if He doesn't. He is not willing to believe that God has a right to treasure up His bright designs, but rather he insists that God must make his bright designs known and understandable to him when and how he chooses. The proud man does judge the Lord by feeble sense and will not trust Him for His grace. The proud man takes it upon himself to interpret what God is doing and will not allow God to be his own interpreter at such a time and in such a way as He chooses. Not so for the truly humble man.

How Do We Measure Up?

As we consider these ten ways that humility manifests itself before God, we must evaluate ourselves. Are these things true of us to a large extent, to some extent, or to any extent? Which of them are lacking in our lives altogether? It is vital that we do more than store this knowledge in our minds. We must allow it to convict us and to change us.

There are areas of pride in all our lives that we need to recognize and deal with, and we must take these things seriously because the only way that we can be useful in the kingdom of God is by being humble servants. God will not use proud people to accomplish His purposes because He is jealous for the glory that belongs to Him. Before going on, look back over these ten manifestations of true humility and pray earnestly to God for help in becoming more humble before Him.

APPLICATION/DISCUSSION EXERCISES

1. Take the following True Humility Inventory, which is designed to evaluate our pride and humility quotient. Since humility is considered by God to be such an important quality and since we are so prone to be proud, this inventory can be helpful in promoting spiritual growth in our lives. Read through each of the manifestations of humility, and then honestly rate yourself using the following rating scale:

   4 = usually true of you;   3 = frequently true of you;
   2 = sometimes;   1 = seldom;   0 = never

   On the items for which you recognized your lack of humility, confess that lack to God as a sin and ask Him for help to change. Periodically, come back and complete this inventory again to evaluate your spiritual growth. Perhaps you would like to ask an honest, brave, and loving friend to rate you on these items as well.

True Humility Inventory
(regarding your behavior before God)

   a. I heartily and freely acknowledge my insignificance and littleness before God._____

   b. I freely confess my sinfulness and unworthiness to God and acknowledge that I am totally unworthy of His mercy and grace._____

c. I am distrustful of myself (Isa. 2:22; Jer. 17:5–6) and know that ultimately I can put my complete and absolute trust only in God (Jer. 17:7–8)._____

d. I renounce all the glory of the good I possess and do, and give God all the glory and credit (Ps. 115:3)._____

e. I am respectful of and receptive, responsive, and obedient to God's Word even when it tells me to do what is difficult and contrary to my own opinion or the opinion of others (Luke 9:23–24)._____

f. I accept and submit myself to God's revealed will even if it is difficult and might cause others to criticize me and lose respect for me when I do so (Matt. 5:5, 10–12)._____

g. I am content with the providence and daily provisions of God for my life (Phil. 4:10–13; Heb. 13:5–6)._____

h. I delight in worshiping and praising God (Ps. 34:1–3; Ps. 108:1–5; Phil. 3:3;)._____

i. I am continually seeking God in prayer (Luke 18:1; Phil. 4:6; 1 Thess. 5:17)._____

j. I consider it a great privilege to serve Christ in small, insignificant, and unnoticed things—basin-and-towel things—as well as tasks that are considered by others to be important and that bring recognition._____

k. I am content to acknowledge God's superiority of wisdom and knowledge; I don't require God to explain to me whatever He is doing; I rest in His wisdom and love and grace when the reasons for events and circumstances are not clear to me (Deut. 29:29; Rom. 11:32–36)._____

l. I realize that God doesn't owe me anything except hell and that any pleasures I experience in this life are wholly undeserved._____

m. When I experience suffering or unpleasantness, I don't get upset or bitter with God; nor do I think or say, "How could God ever allow this to happen to me? God isn't treating me as well as I should be treated. I don't deserve this. I've tried to serve Him, I've read my Bible and prayed faithfully, I've gone to church regularly, I've given to Him, I've witnessed. I've tried to be moral. God should treat me better than this."_____

2. In your estimation, what were the most challenging and helpful things that were stated in this chapter on humility? What was the most meaningful of the ten manifestations of true humility presented in this chapter?

3. Look up the following verses and notice the different ways in which our Lord Jesus Christ displayed humility: Matthew 11:25–30; 20:25–28; Luke 2:7; 10:21–22; Philippians 2:5–8.

4. Look up the following verses and note the warnings God gives to the proud and the promises God makes to those who are humble: Psalms 9:12; 10:17; 25:9; 149:4; Proverbs 3:34; 10:17; 15:33; 16:19; 22:4; 29:23; Isaiah 57:15; 66:1–2; Matthew 20:26–27; 1 Peter 5:5–7.

5. Study the following verses and write down how true humility displayed itself or should display itself: Exodus 34:5–8; 2 Kings 22:8–13; Psalms 81:1–5; 115:1–3; Acts 5:41–42; 10:30–33; 17:10–12; 1 Corinthians 4:6–7; 15:9–10; 2 Corinthians 3:4–7; Ephesians 4:1; Philippians 1:10–12; Colossians 4:12; 1 Timothy 1:12–16; James 1:21; Revelation 1:12–17.

3

PORTRAIT OF HUMILITY TOWARD MAN

In our world, pride is almost always considered an admirable trait. People are proud of their nationality, proud of their positions, proud of their sports teams, and even proud of their honor students. The United States citizen is "Proud to be an American." The gay community has adopted pride as part of its motto. It would seem that everyone is proud of something . . . and proud of it!

This was confirmed to me by a quick Internet search on the word "pride." I found that Web site after Web site presented pride as a positive, commendable thing. And while there certainly is a sense in which pride can be good when it is used to mean self-respect or thinking positively about something that you stand for, it is increasingly apparent that our world has lost touch with the idea that pride can be a very destructive and evil thing. Indeed, it would seem that the only evil associated with pride these days is either to not have it or to destroy someone else's.

As we have already noted, God does not think as the world does when it comes to pride. In Proverbs 6:16–19 we learn that pride is one of the seven things that are an abomination to Him. Here are some more passages of Scripture that describe God's opinion of pride:

> Pride and arrogance and the evil way and the perverted mouth, I hate. (Prov. 8:13)

> The LORD will tear down the house of the proud. . . . (Prov. 15:25)

> Haughty eyes and a proud heart, the lamp of the wicked, is sin. (Prov. 21:4)

> Do you see a man wise in his own eyes? There is more hope for a fool than for him. (Prov. 26:12)

> "Behold, I am against you, O arrogant one," declares the Lord GOD of hosts. . . . (Jer. 50:31)

> "Whoever exalts himself shall be humbled. . . ." (Matt. 23:12)

> For if anyone thinks he is something when he is nothing, he deceives himself. (Gal. 6:3)

> God is opposed to the proud. . . . (James 4:6)

Over the years of church history, other well-known Christians have commented on pride in this manner. As previously noted, Saint Chrystostom said that pride is the mother of all evils."[1] Amy Carmichael, a longtime missionary to the people of India, said, "Those who think too much of themselves don't think enough."[2] Thomas Watson wrote:

> Man is naturally a proud piece of flesh. This sin runs in the blood, but the godly do not allow themselves in it. Our first parents fell by their pride. They aspired to deity. There are the seeds of this in the best of us, but the godly do not allow themselves in it. They strive to kill this weed of pride by mortification. But certainly where this sin reigns and prevails, it cannot stand with grace. You may as well call him who lacks discretion a prudent man, as him who lacks humility a godly man. . . . It is better to lack anything than humility. It is better to lack gifts rather than humility. No, it is better to lack "the comforts of the Spirit" than lack humility.[3]

The great preacher Charles Spurgeon said this about pride:

> I must try to describe pride to you. I might paint it as being the worst malformation of all the monstrous things in creation. It has nothing lovely in it, nothing in proportion, but everything in disorder. It is altogether the very reverse of the creatures which God has made, which are pure and holy. Pride is the first-born son of hell. It is indeed like its parent, all unclean and vile, and in it there is neither form, fashion, or comeliness. Pride is a groundless thing; it stands on the sands, or worse than that, it puts its foot on the billows which yield beneath its tread. Or worse still, it

stands on bubbles, which soon must burst beneath its feet. Of all things, pride has the worst foothold. It has no solid rock on earth whereon to place itself. We have reasons for almost everything, but we have no reasons for pride. Pride is a thing which should be unnatural to us, for we have nothing to be proud of.[4]

And C. S. Lewis once proposed that if humility is the most important Christian virtue, then pride is the greatest sin:

> There is one vice of which no man in the world is free, which everyone in the world loathes when he sees it in someone else, and which hardly any people except Christians ever imagine that they are guilty of themselves. The only people who do not see it that way are Christians. There is no fault that makes a man more unpopular, no fault which we are more conscious of in ourselves. And the more we have it in ourselves, the more we dislike it in others. According to the Christian teachers, the essential vice, the utmost evil, is pride. Unchastity (unfaithfulness), anger, greed, drunkenness, and all that are mere flea bites in comparison. It was through pride that the devil became the devil. Pride leads to every other vice. It is a completely anti-God state of mind.[5]

The world may think that pride is an admirable trait, but clearly the Word of God and many godly teachers of the Word agree that pride is a wicked and horrible thing that needs to be eliminated from our lives.

Having considered in the last chapter how humility displays itself before God, we will now focus on the way in which humility manifests itself before other people. In other words, how does true humility influence our attitude toward and behavior before other people? As we look at the answer to this question, we must continue to think about and honestly answer another question: Are these things true of me?

No doubt we will find that there are indeed areas of pride in our lives. When the Holy Spirit convicts us of our sinful pride, we must be prepared to stop immediately and deal with it. We must repent, go to the cross and confess our sins, and ask God for forgiveness. We then must humbly ask for the Holy Spirit's help in bringing about change in our lives.

A PORTRAIT OF A TRULY HUMBLE PERSON

What does a truly humble person look like to others? True humility has many aspects, and we will consider each of them in the next two chapters as we seek to put together a verbal picture of the truly humble person.

First, a truly humble person is not selfishly ambitious and greedy of honor among or over other people. James 3:14–16 warns, "But if you have bitter jealousy and selfish ambition in your heart, do not be arrogant and so lie against the truth. This wisdom is not that which comes down from above, but is earthly, natural, demonic. For where jealousy and selfish ambition exist, there is disorder and every evil thing." Bitter jealousy and selfish ambition toward other people are both attitudes that flow out of a heart that is not interested in glorifying God, but rather in glorifying self. We cannot claim to love God and desire His glory if we are coveting what someone else has or are seeking our own gain.

An excellent example of a person who did not display this kind of humility before others is Baruch, the *amanuensis* (secretary) of the prophet Jeremiah. While we are not told in the Scripture exactly what the source of Baruch's pride was, it seems likely that he became puffed up with the idea that he was honored to be the one recording the Word of God through Jeremiah. While it is true that Baruch was performing a very important task, the greatness of the task did not make him, the person who performed it, great.

It appears that instead of recording the Word of God through Jeremiah for the glory of God, Baruch was performing this service for the glory of himself. Jeremiah, understanding Baruch's heart, rebuked him for this display of pride. " 'But you, are you seeking great things for yourself? Do not seek them . . .' " (Jer. 45:5). Baruch was selfishly ambitious. He was seeking honor for himself rather than for God.

Third John provides another example of a person who was selfishly ambitious and seeking honor among people. In this passage we learn that a man named Diotrephes was a leader in one of the early churches, perhaps a pastor or elder. John wrote of him:

> I wrote something to the church; but Diotrephes, who loves to be first among them, does not accept what we say. For this reason, if I come, I will call attention to his deeds which he does, unjustly accusing us with wicked words; and not satisfied with this, he himself

does not receive the brethren, either, and he forbids those who desire to do so and puts them out of the church.

Beloved, do not imitate what is evil, but what is good. The one who does good is of God; the one who does evil has not seen God. (3 John 9–11)

Wanting to be first and to be regarded most highly by the people in his church, this man refused to accept the inspired writing and teaching of the apostle John. Perhaps something that John had written contradicted this man's teaching to his local church. From what John wrote in this letter, we see that Diotrephes was responding to this problem by slandering John and the other apostles.

When we slander other people, it is usually because of our pride. Putting others down makes us look better. But not only was this man slandering the apostles in order to make himself look better, he was also excommunicating people from the church for wrong reasons. His selfish ambition and his desire to run everyone else's lives led to serious abuse of his authority as an elder in the church. He was deciding with whom his congregation could and could not fellowship and cutting off those who did not listen to him.

John urged his readers not to imitate the example of this evil man and then gave them an example of a truly humble person to imitate instead: "Demetrius has received a good testimony from everyone, and from the truth itself; and we add our testimony, and you know that our testimony is true" (3 John 12). In other words, Demetrius was a man whose life bore witness to his godliness, and everyone—including the apostles—recognized it.

Haman, in the book of Esther, is another example of a proud person who had great selfish ambition. In Esther 3, the Scripture tells us that King Ahasuerus promoted Haman to a very high position in the kingdom. As a result, all the king's servants began to bow to Haman whenever they saw him, according to the command of the king:

> All the king's servants who were at the king's gate bowed down and paid homage to Haman; for so the king had commanded concerning him. But Mordecai neither bowed down nor paid homage. Then the king's servants who were at the king's gate said to Mordecai, "Why are you transgressing the king's command?" Now it was when they had spoken daily to him and he would not listen to them, that they told Haman to see whether Mordecai's reason would stand; for he had told them that he was a Jew. When Haman saw that Mordecai neither bowed down nor paid homage to him, Haman was filled with rage. (Est. 3:2–5)

The extent of Haman's pride was made evident by the fact that he was enraged when someone refused to honor him. How often do we expect to be treated in a certain way because of our position, our age, or our knowledge? How we respond when we are not given the honor that we expect is a good indication of how much pride we have in our hearts. Haman had so much pride (and so much anger as a result) that he convinced the king to issue an edict commanding that all Jews were to be killed at a certain time (Est. 3:8–15).

We see further evidence of Haman's pride later in chapter 5. After enjoying a private banquet with the king and queen, Haman went out into the streets feeling very good about himself. There he encountered Mordecai, who refused to bow to him as usual. This enraged Haman again:

> Haman controlled himself, however, went to his house and sent for his friends and his wife Zeresh. Then Haman recounted to them the glory of his riches, and the number of his sons, and every instance where the king had magnified him and how he had promoted him above the princes and servants of the king. Haman also said, "Even Esther the queen let no one but me come with the king to the banquet which she had prepared; and tomorrow also I am invited by her with the king." (Est. 5:10–12)

Haman was so proud that he invited his friends over just so that he could boast to them about how wonderful he was and how much the king had honored him. Proverbs 27:2 teaches, "Let another praise you, and not your own mouth; a stranger, and not your own lips." Haman, however, delighted in telling others how great he was. He was selfishly ambitious and greedy for honor because of his great pride.

In contrast, Romans 12:16 gives us a picture of what a humble person's attitude and behavior should be before other people: "Be of the same mind toward one another; do not be haughty in mind, but associate with the lowly. Do not be wise in your own estimation."

First, we are taught to "be of the same mind toward one another; do not be haughty in mind." This means that we are to have the same attitude toward everyone else that we have toward ourselves. In other words, we are to love our neighbors just as we love ourselves, as Jesus taught in Matthew 19:19. Our attitude toward ourselves should not be that we are better than anyone else, but rather that we are *no better* than anyone else.

Second, we are commanded to "associate with the lowly." Often, our pride manifests itself in the choice of people with whom we choose to associate. We might prefer to associate with people who are wealthy, are popular, have interesting personalities, dress well, or have a good education. The people with whom we are willing to spend our time are often an indication of what we think of ourselves: who we think we are or who we would like to be.

Jesus once told a story that rebuked this kind of thinking:

> And He also went on to say to the one who had invited Him, "When you give a luncheon or a dinner, do not invite your friends or your brothers or your relatives or rich neighbors, otherwise they may also invite you in return and that will be your repayment. But when you give a reception, invite the poor, the crippled, the lame, the blind, and you will be blessed, since they do not have the means to repay you; for you will be repaid at the resurrection of the righteous." (Luke 14:12–14)

In interpreting this passage, we must first recognize that Jesus was not telling us never to host our friends, relatives, or rich people. As we look at this teaching in the larger context of all of Scripture, I believe that we may read Jesus' words as "do not merely" invite those people. He knows that we will naturally spend time with our friends and relatives, but we must be careful that we do not spend all our time only with those people, ignoring the people who are in need.

If we take the time to stop and evaluate ourselves, we will probably realize that we are all guilty of this kind of pride. How often do we pass a slum or other poor area of town and think to ourselves, "I'm glad I don't live there"? How often do we see a poorly dressed person walking through town and think to ourselves, "I'm glad I don't have to dress like that"? When we think like this, what we are really saying is, "I'm better than they are because my house is nicer and my clothes are nicer." That kind of thinking is a manifestation of pride.

Though we tend to think of riches as material things, people can be rich or poor in other ways as well. Some people are very rich in personality. They are fun to be with and interesting to talk to. Others are as stimulating as a wet noodle. They are difficult to talk to, they make us feel uncomfortable, and we cannot find anything that we have in common with them. A proud person will avoid spending time with such a person because he is more concerned about his own comfort than the other person's need for fellowship.

A humble person, on the other hand, makes an effort to talk to all kinds of people, regardless of how uncomfortable it may be, because a humble person is more concerned about others than he is about himself. Second Corinthians 5:9 says, "Therefore we also have as our ambition, whether at home or absent, to be pleasing to Him." Humble people are more concerned about serving others in order to serve

Christ. They are more concerned about pleasing Christ than pleasing themselves.

One of my heroes of the faith is the man John the Baptist. John the Baptist was a truly humble person in many ways, and I am often challenged by the display of humility in his life. John 1 records one such display that I find especially compelling.

John 1:19 says, "This is the testimony of John, when the Jews sent to him priests and Levites from Jerusalem to ask him, 'Who are you?' " What would our response to such a question be? We would probably talk about our family, our occupation, and our education. John could certainly have given his questioners a similar answer. As the son of one of the most eminent priests of the day, Zechariah, he had an impressive pedigree. He could have told them all about his training and education as a future priest.

What I find so interesting, however, is John's response. Instead of telling the men who he *was*, he told them who he *was not*. John replied simply, " 'I am not the Christ' " (John 1:20). The priests were not satisfied with this answer, and so they continued to question him. They asked if he was Elijah or the Prophet. Again, John said, "No." He continued to identify himself only in terms of who he was not, not who he was. How often, when someone asks us about ourselves, do we reply in terms of what we are not? Do we not love to brag instead about what we have done, where we were educated, and the positions we have held?

Still not satisfied, the men who were questioning John asked, " 'Who are you, so that we may give an answer to those who sent us? What do you say about yourself?' " (John 1:22). John replied to them, " 'I am a voice of one crying in the wilderness, "Make straight the way of the LORD," as Isaiah the prophet said. . . . I baptize in water, but among you stands One whom you do not know. It is He who comes after me, the thong of whose sandal I am not worthy to untie' " (John 1:23–27). John turned their attention away from himself and toward Jesus. That is true humility.

John the Baptist was not selfishly ambitious. He did not seek out honor for himself. He did not care what other people thought about him or who he was. His life was all about giving glory and honor to Jesus Christ, and that is what our lives should be about as well.

The second way in which true humility displays itself before people is by not being ostentatious. In other words, a truly humble person is not a show-off. First Corinthians 13:4 teaches that "love does not brag and is not arrogant." Paul explained this idea in 1 Timothy 2:9–10: "Likewise, I want women to adorn themselves with proper clothing, modestly and discreetly, not with braided hair and gold or pearls or costly garments, but rather by means of good works, as is proper for women making a claim to godliness."

Paul was teaching us that women should focus on their inner character, not their outer adornment. It is not wrong for a woman to fix her hair or wear nice clothes. It *is* wrong for a woman to make those things the basis of her acceptance and importance. When our appearance is showy for the purpose of making us stand out to other people, then our appearance manifests pride. A truly humble person, on the other hand, will dress in such a way so as not to call attention to himself. In our day, that means not deliberately dressing sloppily or immodestly.

Proverbs 7 describes very well what an ostentatious person, or a person who focuses on making a display before others, looks like: "For at the window of my house I looked out through my lattice, and I saw among the naïve, and discerned among the youths a young man lacking sense . . . and behold, a woman comes to meet him, dressed as a harlot and cunning of heart. She is boisterous and rebellious, her feet do not remain at home; she is now in the streets, now in the squares, and lurks by every corner" (Prov. 7:6–7, 10–12). The woman in this passage is an ostentatious person. She is "boisterous"—loud, raucous, the life of the party—and "rebellious"—argumentative and contentious. In other words, she wants to be the center of everyone's attention. That is a manifestation of pride.

I remember counseling a woman at the Christian Counseling and Educational Foundation many years ago. Before I met her, I read through the personal data inventory that she had filled out. In response to the survey question, "What's your problem?" she had written, "Wherever I go, men are always hitting on me." As I went down the stairs to the waiting room, I could smell this woman's perfume even before I saw her. As we went upstairs to my office, I noticed that she had trouble walking up the stairs because her dress was so tight. Though this woman was not yet ready to admit her pride problem, the reason for her attention problem was obvious: she was inviting men's attention by her ostentatious appearance.

The apostle Peter echoed this teaching of Paul in 1 Peter 3:3–4: "Your adornment must not be merely external—braiding the hair, and wearing gold jewelry, or putting on dresses; but let it be the hidden person of the heart, with the imperishable quality of a gentle and quiet spirit, which is precious in the sight of God." The message of Scripture is consistent: as much as possible, we should strive to dress and act in such a way so as to *not* call attention to ourselves.

This teaching goes for men as well as for women. Nowadays, both men and women call attention to themselves with body piercings, tattoos, dyed hair, sloppy clothes, and immodest dress. As Christians, we should aim to evoke neither shock at nor great admiration for our appearance. Rather, our humble spirit should be evident in our unassuming appearance. If people are drawn to us or notice us for any reason, it should be only because we magnify Christ's character in a way that they are not used to seeing in the world around them.

But there is more to being ostentatious than just appearance. Jesus described the ostentatious lives of the Pharisees in Matthew 6. These men were showy in their self-righteousness and practice of religion. Jesus said:

> "Beware of practicing your righteousness before men to be noticed by them; otherwise you have no reward with your Father who is in heaven.
>
> "So when you give to the poor, do not sound a trumpet before you, as the hypocrites do in the synagogues and in the streets, so that they may be honored by men. Truly I say to you, they have their reward in full. . . .
>
> "When you pray, you are not to be like the hypocrites; for they love to stand and pray in the synagogues and on the street corners so that they may be

seen by men. Truly I say to you, they have their reward in full." (Matt. 6:1–2, 5)

It is important to notice the words that Jesus used in this passage. Jesus rebuked the Pharisees not for practicing their righteousness before men; that is exactly what we *should* be doing. People ought to see our righteousness daily. No, Jesus rebuked them for this: practicing their righteousness before men *to be noticed by them*.

Motive is the key in this case. If we pray only in prayer meeting, where others can hear us, then we are being ostentatious. If we read our Bibles only when other people are around to see us doing it, then we are manifesting a proud heart that is concerned only with appearances. If we give only when others will see us giving, then we are not giving to honor Christ but to honor and draw attention to ourselves.

Jonathan Edwards, in his great exposition of 1 Corinthians 13:4–5, wrote:

> If the truly humble man has any advantage or benefit of any kind, either temporal or spiritual above his neighbors, he will not make a show of it. If he has greater natural abilities than others, he will not be forward to parade and display them, or be careful that others should know his superiority in this respect. If he has a remarkable spiritual experience, he will not be solicitous that men should know it, for the sake of the honor he may obtain by it. Nor does he affect to be esteemed of men, as an eminent saint or a faithful servant of heaven. For it is a small thing with him what men may think of him. If he does anything well, or

does his duty in any respect with difficulty and self-denial, he does not affect that men should take notice of it. Nor is he careful, lest they should not observe it. He is not of the behavior of the Pharisees, who, it is said (Matt. 23:5) did all their works to be seen of men; but if he has done anything in sincerity, he is content that the great Being who sees in secret beholds and will approve it.[6]

A truly humble person is not ostentatious around other people. Instead, a truly humble person will be like the apostle Paul, who said, "If I have to boast, I will boast of what pertains to my weakness" (2 Cor. 11:30). Though Paul was used by God to write epistles of the Word of God, do miracles, evangelize thousands, and disciple future leaders of the church, all Paul wanted to do was to talk about his weaknesses because his weaknesses gave God all the glory. A truly humble person wants nothing more than to give God all the glory for everything.

CONCLUSION

We have looked at only two ways in which pride manifests itself before other people: by being selfishly ambitious and greedy for honor and by being ostentatious. In the next chapter we will learn about five more ways that pride manifests itself before others. Before continuing, take a moment to evaluate yourself in light of these two things. And as you think about your own life, remember what God says about the wickedness of pride and the blessing of humility. Pride is not a sin to be taken lightly. We must be eager to root it out and diligent to destroy it because "God is opposed to the proud, but gives grace to the humble" (James 4:6).

APPLICATION/DISCUSSION EXERCISES

1. In your estimation, what were the most challenging and helpful things that were stated in this chapter on humility? Of the two manifestations of humility presented in this chapter, which one was more meaningful to you?

2. Study the following verses and write down how true humility or pride displayed itself: Matthew 6:1–6; 8:1–4; 9:18–28; 20:20–24; 23:1–12; Luke 8:8–14; John 3:22–30; 5:1–13; 8:30–32; James 3:14–16.

3. Think back over the last week, the last month, and the last six months and write down when you've been tempted to be selfishly ambitious and greedy of honor.

4. Think back over the last week, the last month, and the last six months and write down when you've been tempted to be a show-off around people, when you've tried to impress people with your greatness.

4

COMPLETED PORTRAIT OF HUMILITY

Jonathan Edwards once said, "Nothing sets a Christian so much out of the devil's reach than humility."[1] At the beginning of the last chapter, we reviewed the Bible's teaching on God's opinion of pride in contrast to the world's opinion of pride. We saw also that many great teachers of the Bible, godly men and women, have expressed the same disgust for pride that God has in His Word.

Though the Scripture is clear in its condemnation of pride, the Bible also has many positive things to say about the quality of humility. Psalm 25:9 says, "He leads the humble in justice, and He teaches the humble His way." Psalm 37:11 teaches, "But the humble will inherit the land and will delight themselves in abundant prosperity." Psalm 138:6 says, "For though the LORD is exalted, yet He regards the lowly. . . ." In other passages we learn that God lifts up the humble, beautifies the humble, gives grace to the humble, honors the humble, dwells and makes His home with the humble, and blesses the humble.

Charles Spurgeon once said, "Humility is a grace that has many promises given to it in the Scripture. Perhaps most promises are given to faith, and love is often considered to be the brightest of the train of virtues, yet humility holds by no means an inferior place in God's Word. Every grace seems to be like a nail on which precious blessings hang, and humility has many a mercy suspended from it."[2]

As Spurgeon noted, a search of the Scripture reveals that while not one positive promise is given to proud people, many promises of blessing are given to humble people. Knowing this, how can we—if we truly love God and desire to please Him—not pursue this quality in our lives? But how can we know what it means to be humble if we do not understand humility in the way God understands it? And how can we know if we are proud unless we understand it from God's perspective?

It is relatively easy for us to talk about pride and humility and not know what God means by either one. In fact, the Bible warns that many proud people do not even know that they are proud: "All the ways of a man are clean in his own sight, but the LORD weighs the motives" (Prov. 16:2). Pride causes us to overlook our sins and to think more highly of ourselves than we ought.

On the other hand, if we wish to be blessed because of our humility, we *must* understand God's view of that virtue. In the last chapter, we started to look at the way in which humility manifests itself before other people. We learned that a truly humble person is not selfishly ambitious or greedy for honor and that a humble person is not ostentatious around other people. In this chapter we will complete the portrait of a truly humble person with five more characteristics.

Third, a truly humble person is not arrogant and assuming in his relationships with people. Again, we can look at the life of Haman and see what an arrogant and assuming person looks like. In Esther 6, we read that Haman was called before the king: "So Haman came in and the king said to him, 'What is to be done for the man whom the king desires to honor?' And Haman said to himself, 'Whom would the king desire to honor more than me?' " (Est. 6:6). Right away, we see Haman's pride. He immediately assumed that he was the only person whom the king could possibly wish to honor.

A truly humble person is also not like the people described by Paul in Romans 1:21, those who "did not honor . . . God or give thanks." Proud people are critical and do not give honor to anyone, even God. They are not thankful to others when they receive something because they assume that they deserve whatever they get. Proverbs 30:15–16 describes these kinds of people as being like leeches, death, and fire: they are never satisfied. They always want more, and they always assume that they are entitled to more.

Numbers 14 describes how the Israelites were arrogant and assuming toward their leaders: "Then all the congregation lifted up their voices and cried, and the people wept that night" (Num. 14:1). At this point, God's people were not repenting of sin or mourning some great tragedy. They were complaining that Moses and Aaron had led them into a barren land with no food or water: "All the sons of Israel grumbled against Moses and Aaron; and the whole congregation said to them, 'Would that we had died in the land of Egypt! Or would that we had died in this wilderness!' " (Num. 14:2).

They complained and criticized because they assumed that they deserved better leaders and a better life than what they had at present. Pride says, "I deserve better."

Conversely, a truly humble person is like David in 1 Samuel 18:17–23. King Saul offered to David his older daughter, Merab, in marriage. Saul expected David to be honored by this offer, though he desired the marriage only as a means to get David killed by the Philistines. David, however, apparently did not perceive Saul's true motives and humbly responded, " 'Who am I, and what is my life or my father's family in Israel, that I should be the king's son-in-law?' " (18:18).

When Saul later offered the hand of his daughter Michal, David's response was much the same: " 'Is it trivial in your sight to become the king's son-in-law, since I am a poor man and lightly esteemed?' " (18:23). David demonstrated his humility by his inability to imagine himself worthy of the honor of becoming the king's son-in-law. A truly humble person, such as David, does not have an inflated view of himself and assumes that he deserves nothing from anyone.

A humble person, who is not arrogant and assuming, is like Agur, who wrote in Proverbs 30:2–3, "Surely I am more stupid than any man, and I do not have the understanding of a man. Neither have I learned wisdom, nor do I have the knowledge of the Holy One." He is also like Paul, who declared in 1 Corinthians 15:9, "For I am the least of the apostles, and not fit to be called an apostle, because I persecuted the church of God." More than that, Paul viewed himself as "the very least of all saints" (Eph. 3:8) because he was a truly humble man. Humble people are not arrogant or assuming in their relationships with others.

Fourth, a truly humble person is not scornful of, contentious with, or violent toward other people. Again, Haman demonstrated the opposite of this kind of humility. He assumed that others should worship him, he considered himself deserving of the respect of others, and he became enraged when he did not receive what he thought he deserved. In fact, he was so angry with Mordecai for not bowing down to him that he had a gallows built on which he could hang Mordecai (Est. 5:9–14). Haman's pride caused him to be violent toward others.

King Saul is another example of a very proud person. Twice, when overcome with jealousy toward David, Saul picked up his spear and threw it at David (1 Sam. 18–19). When Jonathan, Saul's own son, did not give him the respect that he thought he deserved, Saul threw his spear at Jonathan and called him the "son of a rebellious woman" (1 Sam. 20:30–33). Violence toward others is a mark of pride.

Pride and violence are also connected in Psalm 73:6–9:

> Therefore pride is their necklace;
> The garment of violence covers them.
> Their eye bulges from fatness;
> The imaginations of their heart run riot.
> They mock and wickedly speak of oppression;
> They speak from on high.
> They have set their mouth against the heavens,
> And their tongue parades through the earth.

Pride leads to violence and scornfulness. Pride leads to mistreating other people because proud people deem themselves better than others. They see other people as less deserving of respect, comfort, or even life.

Proverbs often describes people who are scornful and contentious. "Through insolence comes nothing but strife . . ." (Prov. 13:10). Someone who is always in fights with others and finding fault with everyone is a proud person. The scornful words of proud people cause others to become angry and stirred up against them. "A worthless man digs up evil, while his words are like scorching fire" (Prov. 16:27). As a result, everyone involved is disgraced. "When pride comes, then comes dishonor . . ." (Prov. 11:2).

A truly humble person, however, as Paul commanded in Ephesians 4:31, will "let all bitterness and wrath and anger and clamor and slander be put away from you, along with all malice." They will also "be kind to one another, tenderhearted, forgiving each other, just as God in Christ also has forgiven you" (Eph. 4:32). Their words will be kind rather than contentious, soothing rather than scornful.

A humble person will follow the example of Christ on the cross when he looked down at those who had humiliated him and blessed them: "But Jesus was saying, 'Father, forgive them; for they do not know what they are doing' " (Luke 23:34). In doing this, Christ demonstrated the words of the apostle Peter in 1 Peter 3:8–9: "To sum up, all of you be harmonious, sympathetic, brotherly, kindhearted, and humble in spirit; not returning evil for evil or insult for insult, but giving a blessing instead. . . ." A proud person insults and stirs up trouble with others, but a humble person is a peacemaker and encourager.

Fifth, a truly humble person is not willful and stubborn in his relationships with people. Second Peter 2:10 talks about people who are "daring" and "self-willed." These are proud people because their own pleasure rules their lives and determines their actions. As Paul wrote, these kinds of people "seek after their own interests, not those of Christ Jesus" (Phil. 2:21). Proud people look out only for "number one" because they esteem themselves more highly than anyone else—even God.

Paul demonstrated his humility in his relationship with others in 1 Corinthians 9. In this chapter, Paul wrote about how he had to defend himself to certain people. These people were criticizing him because they did not like the message that he was bringing. Because of their dislike for what he was teaching, they attempted to discredit the message by attacking the messenger. They were too proud to simply admit that they did not want to accept his commands.

Though Paul certainly had the right to defend himself because of his freedom in Christ, his authority as an apostle, and his ministry (1 Cor. 9:1), he chose to give up those rights for the sake of furthering the gospel: "For though I am free from all men, I have made myself a slave to all, so that I may win more. . . . I do all things for the sake of the gospel, so that I may become a fellow partaker of it" (1 Cor. 9:19, 23). Paul was willing to put himself aside in all things so that others could see Christ: "I also please all men in all things, not seeking my own profit but the profit of the many, so that they may be saved" (1 Cor. 10:33).

Truly humble people are not selfish or willful toward others because they do not seek their own (1 Cor. 13:5). Their lives demonstrate the words of Paul in Philippians 2:3–4: "Do nothing from selfishness or empty conceit, but with humility of mind regard one another as more important than yourselves; do not merely look out for your own personal interests, but also for the interests of others."

Humble people are willing to turn the other cheek, as Jesus commanded in Matthew 5:39, when they are offended or wronged. Conversely, proud people always have to retaliate when they are offended by someone, no matter how small the offense. A slap on the cheek immediately elicits a punch in the nose. The pride in our hearts causes us to jump up to defend ourselves or pay back every slight. A humble person accepts the wound and is even willing to receive more if need be.

In the passage in Matthew 5, Jesus continued by saying, " 'If anyone wants to sue you and take your shirt, let him have your coat also' " (5:40). Humble people are willing to do whatever it takes to smooth over an offense. They are not selfish with themselves, their reputation, their possessions, their time, or their opinions. Jonathan Edwards once said:

> Humility disposes men to be of a yielding spirit toward others. Ready for the sake of peace, and to gratify others, to comply in many things with their inclinations and to yield to their judgments, wherein they are not inconsistent with truth and holiness. A truly humble person is inflexible in nothing but in the cause of his Lord and Master, which is the cause of truth and virtue. In this he is inflexible, because God and conscience require it, but in things of lesser moment, and which do not involve his principles as a follower of Christ, and in things that only concern his own private interests, he is apt to yield to others. And if he sees that oth-

ers are stubborn and unreasonable in their willfulness, he does not allow that to provoke him to be stubborn and willful in his opposition to them, but he rather acts on the principles taught in Rom. 12:19; 1 Cor. 6:7; Matt. 5:40, 41, which says, "Dearly beloved, avenge not yourselves, but rather 'give place unto wrath.' " "Why do ye not rather take wrong? Why do ye not rather suffer yourselves to be defrauded?" "If any man will sue thee at the law, and take away thy coat, let him have thy cloak also. And whosoever shall compel thee to go a mile, go with him twain."[3]

All of this is to say that humble people are not willful in their relationships with others.

Sixth, a truly humble person does not try to level those who are over him down to his own level. This biblical concept about humility means that a truly humble person will show respect for and submit to those whom God has given as authorities over them. They do not attempt to undermine or discredit those in authority, nor do they attempt to escape their responsibility to obey.

Consider this quote from Edwards about true humility:

Some persons are always ready to level those above them down to themselves, while they are never willing to level those below them up to their own position. But he that is under the influence of humility will avoid these extremes . . . [;] he will be willing that all should rise just as far as their diligences and worth of character entitle them to; and . . . he will be willing that his superiors should be known and acknowledged in their place, and have rendered to them all the honors that are their due. He will not desire that all should stand on the same level, for he knows it is best that there be gradations in society; that some should be above others, and should be honored and submitted to as such. . . . He is willing to be content with the divine arrangement. . . ."[4]

Proud people do not submit to the laws of their governments as Romans 13:1 calls us to do: "Every person is to be in subjection to the governing authorities." Proud people fight with their bosses at work and do not show them the respect they deserve, which is contrary to Colossians 3:22: "Slaves, in all things obey those who are your masters on earth, not with external service, as those who merely please men, but with sincerity of heart, fearing the Lord."

Proud children do not honor their parents, proud wives do not submit to their husbands, and proud husbands do not love their wives sacrificially as Paul commanded in Colossians 3:18–20. Proud people do not submit to and give honor to the leadership of their churches as 1 Thessalonians 5:12–13 instructs: "But we request of you, brethren, that you appreciate those who diligently labor among you, and have charge over you in the Lord and give you instruction, and that you esteem them very highly in love because of their work."

The Israelites demonstrated this kind of pride when they rebelled against the leadership of Moses in the wilderness. In Numbers 12:1–3, we read that Aaron and Miriam (the brother and sister of Moses) questioned Moses' role as sole leader over the people. Later, in Numbers 16, Korah and some others stirred up the Israelites against Moses:

And they rose up before Moses, together with some of the sons of Israel, two hundred and fifty leaders of the congregation, chosen in the assembly, men of renown. They assembled together against Moses and Aaron, and said to them, "You have gone far enough, for all the congregation are holy, every one of them, and the LORD is in their midst; so why do you exalt yourselves above the assembly of the LORD?" (Num. 16:2–3)

Because of their pride, the people of Israel assumed that they had as much right to receive honor and be an authority over the people as Moses and Aaron did. Truly humble people will not rebel against those who have been placed in authority over them.

Seventh, a truly humble person is willing to receive and benefit from biblical instruction, biblical rebukes, biblical reproof, and constructive criticism. In fact, the way in which we respond to these kinds of corrections is a very good indication of how proud or humble we are. Proverbs 9:8b–9 says, "Reprove a wise man and he will love you. Give instruction to a wise man and he will be still wiser, teach a righteous man and he will increase his learning." On the other hand, "He who corrects a scoffer gets dishonor for himself, and he who reproves a wicked man gets insults for himself. Do not reprove a scoffer, or he will hate you . . ." (Prov. 9:7–8a).

I experienced a tremendous illustration of this principle while supervising a counseling internship at the Master's College Summer Institute a few years ago. For the internship, the students are videotaped doing some actual counseling. The class then views and critiques each other's counseling technique. The class I was working with that summer consisted of seven men and one woman, five of the men being veteran pastors of twenty to thirty years.

When we met together to critique their counseling, I would give the class some time to make comments and then I would give my feedback, both positive and negative, on what they had done. This time of critique lasted for four hours every day for five days, and by Wednesday I was thinking to myself how much constructive criticism I had been handing out. I thought about the fact that I did not like to be critical of others because, like most other people, I wanted to be liked. At the same time, I had a responsibility to help them be better counselors.

As we sat around at a break on that Wednesday, I said to the group, "You guys are going to hate me. I'm afraid that I'm going to lose some friends because of the fact that I am being very up front with you about the things that I think you've done wrong, and other things that I think you really ought to do." To my great surprise and blessing, they all humbly responded, "No, we love you for doing it! That's why we're here. We want to improve and we want to learn. We appreciate the fact that you are helping us to understand what we're doing wrong and how to do it right." What an example of true humility! Those students really longed for instruction and genuinely loved correction.

In Psalm 141:5 David said, "Let the righteous smite me in kindness and reprove me; it is oil upon the head; do not let my head refuse it. . . ." A mark of true humility is our willingness to be rebuked, corrected, and instructed when we are wrong. A truly humble person welcomes it because he knows that he has a propensity for being sinful and needs help in being righteous.

As we close this chapter, I would like to summarize by taking a quick look at three things that we have broadly considered in the last several chapters: first, how pride and humility differ in respect to our view of ourselves; second, how pride and humility differ in respect to our view of other people; and third, how pride and humility differ in respect to consequences.

In regard to a view of oneself, pride makes self the focus. Proud people think about their needs, their wants, and their reputations. They expect praise from others, and they are blind to their own faults. They are easily offended. Humility, on the other hand, makes God the focus. Humble people think about what pleases God and what His will is. They are willing to be both attacked and critiqued. They overcome evil with good. They desire above all for Jesus to be magnified and themselves to be diminished.

In regard to a view of other people, pride refuses to admit mistakes and never asks to be forgiven. Proud people do not submit to authority; they are disrespectful, slanderous, and rebellious. They blame others and justify themselves. They reject correction or instruction, and they do not listen well. They are self-serving and expect to be served by others. Essentially, proud people have a distorted view of reality; they delude themselves into thinking that they are superior to other people and that they understand other people's thoughts and motives. They trivialize the bad things they have done to others and exaggerate what others have done to them.

Humility, however, seeks godly counsel. Humble people seek out correction and instruction and are quick to admit when they are wrong. They are quick to ask forgiveness, and they graciously submit to authority. Humble people strive to resolve conflict and listen carefully to others. They are thankful when they are rebuked. Humble people seek to help others be more Christlike, and they love to serve others. They speak softly and encourage others. They view others as better than themselves.

One of the consequences of pride is an uncontrolled tongue that lashes out at others. Proud people hurt other people because they are slanderous, gossiping, quarrelsome, and divisive. They alienate people and destroy relationships. Another consequence of pride is being unteachable. Proud people are stubborn, and therefore they remain spiritually immature. Further, pride leads to dishonesty and inconsistency. Proud people cannot be trusted because they do not value the commitments they have made to others. Ultimately, pride robs people of joy, peace, and usefulness for Christ.

The consequences of humility are vastly different because they are all blessings. Humble people grow in grace and are spiritually fruitful. They have close relationships with other people. They receive honor, not because they seek it out, but because the Bible promises that God Himself will honor the humble. Humble people are transformed more and more into the image of Christ. They are dependable, steadfast, and helpful to other people. Most importantly, humble people are able to look forward to the day when they will stand before God and He will say to them, "Well done, thou good and faithful servant."

As you consider this description of pride and humility, what do you see in yourself? Does your life resemble that of the truly humble person or that of the proud person? What areas of your life need to change? If the Holy Spirit is convicting you of pride in your life, do not delay in repenting of this destructive evil. Perhaps you're saying, "All right already; I understand that I do struggle with the problem of pride, and I do want to develop more humility, but how can I do that?" Good question. I hope by this time you're asking that question. And I assure you that in the last two chapters of the book I will answer that question. At that time I will present some practical ways for increasing humility and decreasing pride in our lives. But before we do that, I want to do two other things. First, I want to conclude this chapter by giving you some application and discussion exercises. And then in the next chapter, I want to reemphasize and expand on the folly of pride and the wisdom of humility.

APPLICATION/DISCUSSION EXERCISES

1. Take the following True Humility Inventory, which is designed to evaluate our pride and humility quotient. Since humility is considered by God to be such an important quality and since we are so prone to be proud, this inventory can be helpful in promoting spiritual growth in our lives. Read through each of the manifestations of humility, and then honestly rate yourself using the following rating scale:

   4 = usually true of you; 3 = frequently true of you;
   2 = sometimes; 1 = seldom; 0 = never

   On the items for which you recognized your lack of humility, confess that lack to God as a sin and ask Him for help to change. Periodically, come back and complete this inventory again to evaluate your spiritual growth. Perhaps you would like to ask an honest, brave, and loving friend to rate you on these items as well.

True Humility Inventory
(regarding your behavior toward people)

    a. I am not selfishly ambitious or greedy of the honor and appreciation of men._____

    b. I am not ostentatious around people; I don't try to impress people with my intelligence or abilities or status in life._____

    c. I am not arrogant, assuming, or presumptuous in my behavior toward people._____

    d. I am not scornful of, contemptuous toward, or demeaning to people._____

    e. I am not willful or stubborn in my behavior toward people._____

    f. I don't seek to level those who are over me or have authority over me; I show respect for and am willing to submit to God-ordained authorities._____

    g. I show respect for and am willing to submit to others who are not as educated or gifted as I may be._____

    h. I am not defensive when others rebuke me or criticize me._____

    i. I am willing to confess my sins and faults to others and frequently do so._____

    j. I am willing to accept instruction and correction from others._____

k. I am willing to serve others and not be upset when I don't receive appreciation for what I've done.____

l. It doesn't bother me when others are honored more than I am.____

m. It doesn't bother me when others are honored for something I've done.____

n. I am willing to sacrificially serve others even if they are not willing to serve or help me.____

o. I am willing to sacrificially serve others even if it involves hardship and difficulty.____

p. I am willing to listen to others rather than talk or express my opinion.____

q. I am willing to seek and follow good counsel.____

r. When I must make decisions, I seek the input and perspectives of others before acting.____

s. I display a lifestyle of truthfulness even if others may be upset with me for telling the truth about what I have done or said.____

t. I am Christlike in my attitude, words, and actions toward others.____

2. In your estimation, what were the most challenging and helpful things that were stated in this chapter on humility? Of the five additional manifestations of humility presented in this chapter, which one was the most meaningful to you?

3. Study the following verses and write down how true humility or pride displayed itself: Genesis 13:7–9; 2 Samuel 9:1–8; Proverbs 28:23; 28:13; 13:1; 12:1; 15:12; 27:2; Luke 14:7–11; John 13:1–17; Acts 14:8–15; 18:24–28;

Romans 12:10, 16–21; 15:25–31; 1 Corinthians 4:6–7; 16:15; Galatians 2:11–15; Ephesians 5:21; Philippians 2:3–4; 17–22; 1 Peter 5:5.

4. Think back over the last few weeks of your life and write down when you've been tempted to be arrogant and assuming in your behavior toward people.

5. Think back over the last few weeks of your life and write down when you've been tempted to be scornful or contemptuous of other people.

6. Think back over the last few weeks of your life and write down when you've been tempted to be willful or stubborn in your relationship with people.

7. Think back over the last few weeks of your life and write down when you've been tempted to level others in authority over you.

8. Think back over the last few weeks of your life and write down when you've been tempted to be defensive.

9. Think back over the last few weeks of your life and write down when you've been tempted to be unwilling to admit your sins and confess them to God and others.

10. Think back over the last few weeks of your life and write down when you've been tempted to be unwilling to submit yourself to other people, unwilling to yield on issues that don't involve biblical principle.

11. Think back over the last few weeks of your life and write down when you've been tempted to be jealous or envious of others.

12. Think back over the last few weeks of your life and write down when you've been tempted to not listen but rather want to be the center of attention as you do the talking.

13. Think back over the last few weeks of your life and write down when you've been tempted to be unwilling to sacrificially serve other people.

14. Think back over the last few weeks of your life and write down when you've been tempted to be dishonest or untruthful in an attempt to avoid the disapproval of other people.

15. Think back over the last few weeks of your life and write down when you've been tempted to be un-Christlike in your attitude, speech, or conduct.

5

THE FOLLY OF PRIDE

Thus far in this book, we have focused on the value of humility and the danger of pride. In this chapter, we want to expand on the theme of the foolishness of pride. We want to do this for the same reason that our government spends millions of dollars warning us of the dangers of smoking. Just as smoking is a destructive—even lethal—habit, so pride is a destructive and lethal sin. It has damned not only Satan and other angels, but many men and women throughout history.

Yet instead of warring against it, our world actually promotes pride. If I delivered a message on the foolishness of pride to a group of unbelievers, I am certain that people would look at me as if *I* were the only fool in the room. After all, we have programs in our schools that are designed to promote pride.

The truth is, many people do not see pride as the ultimate sin. James 4 makes it clear that Satan wants to promote pride and squelch humility. He has strategies for doing this;

one of them is to fan the flames of pride and to stamp out any small spark of humility. For this reason, it is imperative that we fully understand the foolishness of pride.

If we know our hearts, we know that they are prone to pride because pride is natural. Humility is supernatural. As Charles Spurgeon explained, "There is nothing into which the heart of man so easily falls as pride, and yet there is no vice which is more frequently, and emphatically, and more eloquently condemned in Scripture."[1] Or as John Newton once wrote:

> It is easy for me to advise you to be humble, and for you to acknowledge the propriety of the advice; but while human nature remains in its present state, there will be almost the same connection between popularity and pride as between fire and gunpowder, they cannot meet without an explosion, at least not unless the gunpowder is kept very damp.[2]

Though Scripture and even human experience testify to the destructiveness of pride, millions and millions of people ignore the warning every day. It is far too easy to simply give in and go with the flow.

Since the world promotes pride, Satan promotes pride, and our hearts promote pride, it is clear that we are dealing with a very serious and difficult enemy. It is vitally important that we pay careful attention to what God says about pride so that we do not find ourselves ensnared by it.

In prior chapters, we have discussed why it is so foolish for us to have an inflated, exalted opinion of ourselves. In this chapter, we will continue that focus by further exploring some important reasons why pride is a manifestation of foolishness.

THE FOLLY OF PRIDE: GOD'S PERSPECTIVE

First, *it is foolish for us to be proud about ourselves because of God's attitude toward the proud person.* Do you want to know what God hates? Solomon told us in Proverbs 6:17 that God hates a proud look. In Proverbs 16:5, he put it even more bluntly: "Everyone who is proud in heart is an abomination to the LORD." God hates pride because pride is a violation of the first commandment: "You shall have no other gods before Me" (Ex. 20:3).

Pride is self-idolatry. God alone is to be worshiped and served because His will is supreme and He alone is God, but pride asserts that man should take supremacy over God. God proclaimed through Isaiah, "My glory I will not give to another" (Isa. 48:11). God will not tolerate a usurper who attempts to rise above Him. God hates pride because the proud man sets himself up in opposition to God. The proud man attempts to steal the glory that God alone deserves.

This is why James tells us that God is opposed to the proud. When we are proud, we are setting ourselves up in opposition to God. Think about that idea for a moment: you versus God. By any measure, this is not a good match; we have no chance against the Almighty God. As Thomas Watson explained, "The proud man is the mark which God shoots at. And He never misses the mark."[3]

As believers, we have the privilege of being on God's side, which means that we are at peace with him. But when we demonstrate a proud and arrogant attitude, it is as if we are now choosing to play for the other team. Just imagine a basketball game in which one player decides to shoot baskets in the other team's hoop. In the same way, when we are proud, we are "scoring points" for the wrong team—Satan's team.

If we say that we love God, how can we ever be content with doing something that He hates? We cannot. If we are truly believers, we will instead wage war against pride because we understand what Scripture says about God's attitude toward the proud person.

Second, *it is foolish for us to be proud about ourselves because we have no reason apart from Christ to be proud.* What would you think of a person who went around speaking very dogmatically about all sorts of different issues but was always wrong? "Two plus two equals five. The earth is flat." I remember feeling embarrassed when I recently saw someone being asked who was president before Bill Clinton. The woman confidently replied, "Colin Powell." She was so certain of her answer, and yet she was so completely wrong. We feel embarrassed for people when they display their ignorance like that because they are showing everybody just how little they know.

This is exactly what we are doing when we become proud. We are displaying our ignorance; we are showing everyone just how little we really know. When we are proud, we are acting as if we are the Creator when, in fact, we are only His creatures. In other words, we are forgetting our natural insignificance.

Think about some of the things that people are proud about. *People are often proud when they have some power.* They think they are something because they have been placed in a position of authority. Scripture explains that God is the one who gives men power and authority and that He is able to take that power and authority away. Isaiah wrote, "He it is who reduces rulers to nothing, who makes the judges of the earth meaningless" (Isa. 40:23).

In Daniel 4, we learn that King Nebuchadnezzar discovered this truth the hard way. King Nebuchadnezzar had become strong and great and was a person of incredible importance in this world's eyes. But instead of praising and giving glory to God, he began to take pride in himself and in his power, as he himself related:

> "The king reflected and said, 'Is this not Babylon the great, which I myself have built as a royal residence by the might of my power and for the glory of my majesty?' While the word was in the king's mouth, a voice came from heaven, saying, 'King Nebuchadnezzar, to you it is declared: sovereignty has been removed from you, and you will be driven away from mankind, and your dwelling place will be with the beasts of the field. You will be given grass to eat like cattle, and seven periods of time will pass over you until you recognize that the Most High is ruler over the realm of mankind and bestows it on whomever He wishes.' " (Dan. 4:30–32)

The angel's pronouncement was carried out just as it had been proclaimed (Dan. 4:33), and in verses 34–37 we find out what Nebuchadnezzar learned from this experience:

"I blessed the Most High and praised and honored
Him who lives forever;
For His dominion is an everlasting dominion,
And His kingdom endures from generation to
    generation.
"All the inhabitants of the earth are accounted as
    nothing,
But He does according to His will in the host of heaven
And among the inhabitants of earth;
And no one can ward off His hand
Or say to Him, 'What have You done?' . . .

"Now I, Nebuchadnezzar, praise, exalt and honor the
King of heaven, for all His works are true and His ways
just, and He is able to humble those who walk in
pride."

Daniel summed up Nebuchadnezzar's lesson in pride and
humility as he spoke to his son, Belshazzar:

"O king, the Most High God granted sovereignty,
grandeur, glory and majesty to Nebuchadnezzar your
father. Because of the grandeur which He bestowed
on him, all the peoples, nations and men of every language feared and trembled before him. . . . But when
his heart was lifted up and his spirit became so proud
that he behaved arrogantly, he was deposed from his
royal throne and his glory was taken away from him
. . . until he recognized that the Most High God is
ruler over the realm of mankind and that He sets over
it whomever He wishes." (Dan. 5:18–21)

This is a tremendous example of why we should not be proud when we have been given some power and authority. The lesson of King Nebuchadnezzar's life is that any position or prestige that we have gained is from the hand of God, and He could very easily take it away in an instant if He so chose.

People are often proud about their talents and abilities. Someone who is a good basketball player may walk with a little swagger because he or she can play basketball better than others can. A good mechanic may be proud because he knows how to fix cars well. An excellent cook may boast about her skills in the kitchen. We all know that when we have a talent or ability, one of the first things we tend to do is to look around to see whether anyone else has noticed.

We have no reason to be proud about our talents and abilities, however, because *everything* we have is a gift from God. In fact, we can take this down to the most basic level. Could we imagine a person on life support becoming proud and boasting about how well he is breathing? We might answer, "Okay, I'm glad you're breathing, but don't you see? You're breathing only because you're hooked up to this machine." Everything we have is from God, even our breath. We are *completely dependent.* This is true for everything that we are and do.

In 1 Corinthians 4:7, Paul explained, "For who regards you as superior? What do you have that you did not receive? And if you did receive it, why do you boast as if you had not received it?" When we boast about our gifts, we are lying because we are talking and acting as though we had achieved something that we have not. In reality, we are able to achieve anything only because of God's grace.

John Bunyan illustrated this truth in this way: "Think about a tinkling cymbal. A tinkling cymbal is an instrument of music with which a skillful player can make such melodious and heart-inflaming music, that all who hear him play can scarcely hold from dancing; and yet, behold, the cymbal does not have life, neither does any music come from it, but it sounds beautiful because of the skill of the person that plays it."[4] We can do what we do *only* because God enables us to do it.

It is amazing how insidious a sin pride is, though, because we can even become proud about our spiritual gifts. A preacher can become proud about a sermon he preached on humility. Someone can become proud about the amount of money he put into the offering plate. God hates that kind of pride as well, and we must war against it.

Charles Spurgeon once said:

It is of the utmost importance to us to be kept humble. Consciousness of self-importance is a hateful delusion, but one into which we fall as naturally as weeds grow on a dunghill. We cannot be used of the Lord but that we also dream of personal greatness, we think ourselves almost indispensable to the church, pillars of the cause, and foundations of the temple of God. We are nothings and nobodies, but that we do not think so is very evident, for as soon as we are put on the shelf we begin anxiously to enquire, "How will the work go on without me?" As well might the fly on the coach wheel enquire, "How will the mails be carried without me?" Far better men have been laid in the grave without having brought the Lord's work to a standstill, and shall we fume and fret because for a little season we must lie upon the bed of languishing? God sometimes weakens our strength in a way at the precise juncture when our presence seems most needed to teach us that we are not necessary to God's work, and that when we are most useful, He can easily do without us. If this be the practical lesson, the rough schooling may be easily endured for assuredly it is beyond all things desirable that self should be kept low and the Lord alone be magnified.[5]

When my wife was teaching kindergarten some years ago, she noticed a group of children huddled around one particular boy at school. She was curious to know what they were so excited about, so she asked the boy to come over to her desk. When he did, he showed her a picture of Michael Jordan slamming a basketball. My wife then asked him why the picture was so special. The little boy pointed to Michael Jordan and said, "That's me. That's me playing basketball."

It is clear that that young man had some serious delusions of grandeur, but how often do we think similar thoughts about ourselves? We must not fool ourselves into thinking we are someone that we are not. We are just creatures; we must not think that we are the Creator.

When we become proud, not only are we showing that we are ignorant in reference to our natural and moral insignificance, but we are also showing our ignorance of our spiritual condition. As believers, we sometimes have far too rosy a picture of our spiritual condition apart from Christ. That is a dangerous place to be because we will never appreciate the magnificence of what God has done for us in our salvation until we understand what the Bible says about us before our salvation.

Paul used a choice word in Romans 5:10 to describe who we were before God saved us and apart from His continuing work of grace in our lives. He says that we were God's *enemies*. Think about what that means for a moment.

Before God saved us, *our minds were opposed to God.* As Jonathan Edwards explained, "It is evident that the mind of the unsaved man is naturally averse to thinking about God. And hence, if any thoughts of him be suggested to the mind, they soon go away. Such thoughts are not apt to rest in the minds of natural men."[6] Romans 3:18 says of unbelievers, "There is no fear of God before their eyes."

In other words, unbelievers do not think of God rightly. Before we were saved, we, too, had little regard for God. He was small and contemptible in our eyes. We did not fear Him. We valued our friends' opinions of us and were much more afraid of offending them than we were of displeasing the God who made us.

Before God saved us, *our desires were opposed to God.* Ephesians 2:3 explains, "Among them we too all formerly lived in the lusts of our flesh. . . ." We did not desire God. Thinking about God and His attributes was a chore to us; instead, we desired to do evil. If we look into the unsaved heart, we will not find any passion for the true God, only a passion for self. Prior to salvation, there was not even a spark of desire for God in us. As Paul said, "you were dead in your trespasses and sins" (Eph. 2:1).

Before God saved us, *our wills were opposed to God.* Unsaved people do not love God; they hate Him. We may not see that hatred actually displayed because there are things that restrain that hatred at the present time, such as unbelief or a distorted understanding of who God is. But mark this: unless there is a work of grace in a man's heart, when he sees God for who He really is, he will hate Him. Romans 3:10–11 says, "There is none righteous, not even one; there is none who understands, there is none who seeks for God."

Before God saved us, *our behavior was opposed to God.* Paul wrote in Colossians 1:21 that "you were formerly alienated and hostile in mind, engaged in evil deeds. . . ." As unbelievers, we were actively warring against God by disobeying His commands and attempting to dethrone Him. We were not neutral bystanders; we were God-haters, and we demonstrated that hatred for God by our wicked lives.

Before God saved us, *our worship was opposed to God.* Everyone is a worshiper. Unsaved people worship the creation instead of the Creator. No one, however, can serve two masters. Therefore, when a person worships anyone other than the true God, he is setting himself up as God's enemy.

We need to understand that we were God's enemies prior to salvation. We did not seek Him or love Him. Even our best deeds were filthy rags in His sight, polluted by sin. How foolish it is for us to become proud of ourselves when, apart from Christ, there is nothing good in us. It would be like a small child bragging about the mess he had just made in his diaper. As disgusting as that is, taking pride in what we are or have done is even more disgusting because, without Christ, we would be an abomination to the Lord.

Proud people have an unbiblical view of sin and an unbiblical view of themselves. Believing that we were once

God's enemies helps us to see the greatness of Christ, as Jonathan Edwards explains:

> How wonderful is this love that is manifested in giving Christ to die for us. For this is love to enemies. . . . How wonderful was the love of the Father, in giving such a gift to those who not only could not be profitable to him, but were his enemies and to so great a degree. We had great enmity against Him, yet so did He love us, that He gave His own Son to lay down His life, in order to save our lives, from His own throne there, to be in the form of a servant; and instead of a throne of glory, gave Him to be nailed to the cross, and to be laid in the grave, so that we might be brought to a throne of glory. How wonderful was the love of Christ, in thus exercising dying love towards His enemies. He loved those that hated Him, with hatred sought to take away His life, so as voluntarily to lay down His life that they might have life through Him.[7]

It is foolish to become proud because we have nothing to be proud about apart from Christ. Any physical or spiritual blessings that we enjoy are directly from God's hand; the only thing we can claim as our own is our sin.

THE FOLLY OF PRIDE: ITS FRUITS

Third, *it is foolish for us to become proud about ourselves because of what pride produces*. A joke about rabbits goes like this: Two rabbits are hiding in a bush because they are surrounded by a pack of wolves. One of the rabbits looks at the other and says, "What do you think we should we do? Should we try to escape, or should we wait a couple of minutes until we outnumber them?"

Rabbits reproduce very quickly, and so does pride. Pride is constantly having little babies, but these babies are not cute and cuddly little things; they are monsters. These monsters begin to invade every part of a proud person's life, affecting everything that he thinks and says and does.

In other words, pride has terrible side effects. When deciding whether or not to take a certain medicine, one of the things that most of us consider is the drug's side effects. If the label on the bottle said something like, "Loss of mental capacities, coma, possible death . . . ," most of us would put the bottle down very quickly and refuse to use it. In fact, we'd probably not want to keep it around the house. We'd probably want to destroy it quickly. If we gave pride the same consideration, we would choose to stay away from that as well because Scripture tells us that pride has some terrible side effects.

What are the side effects, or consequences, of pride? First, pride causes us to forget God. God warned the Israelites about this danger in Deuteronomy 8:11–14: "Beware . . . [lest], when you have eaten and are satisfied, and have built good houses and lived in them, and when your herds and your flocks multiply, and your silver and gold multiply, and all that you have multiplies, then your heart will become proud *and you will forget the LORD your God who brought you out from the land of Egypt.* . . ."

Second, pride causes us to make poor decisions. In 2 Kings 14, we learn that Amaziah king of Judah was so proud of his defeat of Edom that he decided to provoke a battle against Israel. Though he was warned against it, Amaziah proceeded and was beaten and captured, and his kingdom was ransacked. Proverbs 14:16 says, "A wise man is cautious and turns away from evil, but a fool is arrogant and careless." Our pride often produces careless, thoughtless actions that hurt others and, in the end, hurt us as well.

Third, pride causes us to act in wicked ways. In 2 Chronicles 26, we read that God enabled King Uzziah to succeed in war, so much so that "his fame spread afar, for he was marvelously helped until he was strong. But when he became strong, his heart was so proud that he acted corruptly, and he was unfaithful to the LORD his God, for he entered the temple of the LORD to burn incense on the altar of incense" (2 Chron. 26:15–16). Pride caused Uzziah to act corruptly, to be disloyal to God, and to lack reverence for God.

Fourth, pride produces ingratitude. 2 Chronicles 32:24–25 says, "In those days Hezekiah became mortally ill; and he prayed to the LORD, and the LORD spoke to him and gave him a sign. But Hezekiah gave no return for the benefit he received, because his heart was proud; therefore wrath came on him and on Judah and Jerusalem." Pride caused Hezekiah to be ungrateful for the healing that he had received from God. Unthankful, complaining people are proud people.

Fifth, pride causes us to sin in our speech. In Psalm 31:18 we read, "Let the lying lips be mute, which speak arrogantly against the righteous with pride and contempt." Pride is connected with lying and slandering others, especially those who do right. Psalm 123:4 links pride with the way we treat others: "Our soul is greatly filled with the scoffing of those who are at ease, and with the contempt of the proud."

Sixth, pride causes us to close our ears to God's Word and to lean on our own understanding. Jeremiah 13:9–10 says, " 'Thus says the LORD, "Just so will I destroy the pride of Judah and the great pride of Jerusalem. This wicked people, who refuse to listen to My words, who walk in the stubbornness of their hearts and have gone after other gods to serve them and to bow down to them, let them be just like this waistband which is totally worthless." ' "

The list of things that pride produces could go on, but we might also consider another list: things that pride *prevents*. Pride keeps us from praying, from reading God's Word, from receiving life-giving rebuke, from seeing our own sin, and from repenting. It prevents us from truly listening to others, from developing deep and meaningful relationships, and from being truly useful in the kingdom of God. These are just a few in a long list of spiritual blessings that are prevented by pride.

Jonathan Edwards summed up this idea well: "Pride is the main handle by which Satan grabs hold of Christian persons and is the chief source of all the mischief that he introduces to clog and hinder the work of God."[8] It is foolish for us to be proud because of the many things that God's Word reveals to us about what pride produces.

Closely connected to this idea is the fourth reason that pride is folly: *It is foolish for us to be proud because of what the Bible reveals are the consequences of pride.* Imagine planning a hike on a difficult trail. If we had never hiked this trail before, we might wisely ask someone who knew the trail to provide us with a map. Suppose this person took the time to draw us a map and even talked us through some of the difficult spots, pitfalls, and hidden dangers. With so much help at our disposal, we would be fools to throw away the map before starting out and to deliberately ignore the warnings and advice that we had been given.

We are all on such a journey—the journey of life—and we have been given an infallible map: the Word of God. This map was written by someone who has not only traveled the road, but created it and owns it. We are blessed beyond measure because we have been shown the way and warned of the dangers by the One who knows our road the best.

Yet how often do we fail to pay attention to what He says? The Scripture warns us that some people will distort true doctrine and even make up their own. Throughout history, many pseudo-Christian groups have done precisely what Scripture warned against; many of the cults of our own time are still not heeding the Bible's warnings. Again and again, for example, the warning of 1 Timothy 4:1–3 has gone unheeded: "But the Spirit explicitly says that in later times some will fall away from the faith, paying attention to deceitful spirits and doctrines of demons, by means of the hypocrisy of liars seared in their own conscience as with a branding iron, men who forbid marriage and advocate abstaining from [certain] foods. . . ."

Many have fallen away from the faith and have invented perversions of Scripture, and many have paid attention to these unbiblical teachings. Sometimes, for whatever reason, people simply choose to do exactly the opposite of what God's Word tells them to do. One example is found in Daniel 4. In this section, we're told that Nebuchadnezzar had a dream.

Then we're told that Daniel interpreted the dream, telling the king exactly what was going to happen and why. We might expect that upon Nebuchadnezzar's hearing Daniel's very clear explanation and warning and after receiving such an explicit and direct rebuke for his sin as well as a detailed description of his punishment, Nebuchadnezzar would immediately repent. Instead, we discover that he ignored the message, continued in his sin, and eventually received the judgment of God just as Daniel had foretold.

It may be easy for us to think, as we look at people involved in the cults that so obviously are distorting the Bible, or at the example of Nebuchadnezzar, or at other people who are caught in weak churches, "How could you be so fooled?" And yet the truth is that the same thing often happens to us because we are so easily ensnared by pride.

We cannot deny that God has been good to us. He has gone to great lengths to warn us of the dangers of pride in His Word, but we need to pay careful attention to the warnings.

The LORD preserves the faithful and fully recompenses the proud doer. (Ps. 31:23)

When pride comes, then comes dishonor. . . .
(Prov. 11:2)

The LORD will tear down the house of the proud. . . .
(Prov. 15:25)

Everyone who is proud in heart is an abomination to the LORD; assuredly, he will not be unpunished.
(Prov. 16:5)

Pride goes before destruction, and a haughty spirit before stumbling. (Prov. 16:18)

A man's pride will bring him low. . . . (Prov. 29:23)

Isaiah 2:11 foretells a day when "the proud look of man will be abased and the loftiness of man will be humbled, and the LORD alone will be exalted in that day." And Jesus said in Luke 14:11 that " 'everyone who exalts himself will be humbled, and he who humbles himself will be exalted.' "

The Scripture makes it very clear that pride will be punished in the end. We may think that we are something for a little while on this earth. We may even deceive a few others into believing it also, but we will never fool God. A day is coming when the proud will stand before God and be humiliated, and the humble will stand before God and be exalted.

Sometimes judgment on proud people comes even while they are still on this earth. Herod is a good example of a man who was immediately judged for an act of great pride. Acts 12:21–23 recounts, "On an appointed day Herod, having put on his royal apparel, took his seat on the rostrum and began delivering an address to them. The people kept crying out, 'The voice of a god and not of a man!' And immediately an angel of the Lord struck him because he did not give God the glory, and he was eaten by worms and died."

If we choose to be proud, we are playing with fire and will suffer the consequences. Scripture makes it very clear that a day is coming when God will humble everyone who is proud. Malachi 4:1 foretells, " 'For behold, the day is coming, burning like a furnace; and all the arrogant and every evildoer will be chaff; and the day that is coming will set them ablaze,' says the LORD of hosts, 'so that it will leave them neither root nor branch.' "

Once again, though, we might look at this idea from the opposite angle. We have talked about the consequences of pride, but we could spend just as much time talking about the many benefits of humility.

To begin, Psalm 34:18 says, "The LORD is near to the brokenhearted and saves those who are crushed in spirit." Psalm 51:17 tells us, "The sacrifices of God are a broken spirit; a broken and a contrite heart, O God, You will not despise." God says in Isaiah 57:15, " 'I dwell on a high and holy place, and also with the contrite and lowly of spirit in order to revive the spirit of the lowly and to revive the heart of the contrite.' " Isaiah 66:2 echoes, " 'To this one I will look, to him who is humble and contrite of spirit, and who trembles at My word.' "

Jesus declared, " 'Blessed are the poor in spirit, for theirs is the kingdom of heaven. Blessed are those who mourn, for they shall be comforted. Blessed are the gentle, for they shall inherit the earth' " (Matt. 5:3–5). Earlier, we saw that James wrote about God's promise to give grace to the humble and to exalt them. Pride is foolish not only because of its terrible consequences but also because it causes us to miss out on the blessings of humility.

Fifth, *it is foolish for us to be proud because pride is a characteristic of the wicked, not the righteous.* If we claim to be Christians, then we are claiming to be followers of God. As His followers, we should exhibit characteristics of the One whom we claim to follow. When we manifest pride, however, we are identifying with the enemy instead.

Pride is not just a mistake or a character flaw; it is sin. Proverbs 21:4 warns, "Haughty eyes and a proud heart, the lamp of the wicked, is sin." In Mark 7:22–23, Jesus tells us that pride is evil and defiles a person. In 1 John 2:16 we read that pride is against God. In Psalm 73, the writer uses pride as a synonym for the wicked.

For this very reason, 2 Timothy 3:2 tells us that one of the marks of the last days is that "men will be lovers of self." It makes no sense for a person who claims to love God and who claims to be concerned about righteousness to exhibit pride. In so doing, he is sinning, defiling himself, actively opposing God, acting like the wicked people around him, and living up to Paul's description of the apostate in the last days.

THE FOLLY OF PRIDE: CHRIST'S EXAMPLE

Sixth, *it is foolish for us to be proud because of how Jesus Christ humbled himself.* Jesus Christ deserved all glory and honor. Hebrews 1:3–12 gives us a wonderful description of Christ's glory:

> He is the radiance of His glory and the exact representation of His nature, and upholds all things by the word of His power. . . .
>
> For to which of the angels did He ever say,
> "You are My Son, today I have begotten You"?
>
> And again,
> "I will be a Father to Him
> And He shall be a Son to Me"?

And when He again brings the firstborn into the
world, He says,
"And let all the angels of God worship Him" . . .

Of the Son He says,
"Your throne, O God, is forever and ever,
And the righteous scepter is the scepter of His kingdom.
You have loved righteousness and hated lawlessness;
Therefore God, Your God, has anointed You
With the oil of gladness above Your companions."

And:

"You, Lord, in the beginning laid the foundation of
     the earth,
And the heavens are the works of Your hands;
They will perish, but You remain . . .
You are the same, and Your years will not come to
     an end."

Christ is God, equivalent in glory, majesty, wisdom, and
every other attribute, yet what did He do? Philippians 2 tells
us that Christ humbled Himself. He emptied Himself, took
the nature of a servant, and was obedient to the Father by
allowing Himself to be crucified for our sin. The God of all
became the servant of all. If Christ, who was perfect, volun-
tarily humbled Himself before His creatures, how much more
should we gladly humble ourselves before others?

Pride is the very height of folly. It is foolish because of God's opinion of pride as an abomination and because we are nothing apart from Christ. It is foolish because of the terrible things that pride produces and the wonderful blessings that pride prevents. It is foolish because it has destructive consequences, because it identifies us with the enemy, and because it is directly opposed to the example of humility that Christ set before us.

One of the things that make pride so dangerous is that it can be so hard for us to spot in ourselves. The very definition of pride is thinking better of ourselves than we really are. It is not surprising, then, that proud people do not usually see their pride. For this reason, it is vitally important that we spend time regularly searching out the pride in our hearts. We must determine that we are going to go against the flow of the world, of Satan, and even of our own hearts in defeating this dreaded enemy of godliness.

APPLICATION/DISCUSSION EXERCISES

1. Review this chapter and write down all the reasons why it is utterly foolish for us to be proud and why being humble is a wise course of action. Be prepared to explain them to someone else and by so doing convince that person of the folly of pride and the wisdom of humility.

2. From everything that was presented in this chapter, identify the most challenging and helpful things in your estimation. What areas of pride or humility presented in this chapter were the most meaningful to you? Explain.

3. As you review this chapter, select five of the Bible verses or passages that were most challenging or helpful to you. Or if you have trouble selecting the most challenging, just select five at random. Write them out. Tell why they would be challenging or helpful in seeking to overcome pride and develop humility. Explain how you could use the truths in this chapter to help someone struggling with pride.

4. Select at least one Bible verse and work on committing it to memory.

6

YES, BUT HOW?

Perhaps by this point you find yourself thinking, "I know what the Bible says about the sinfulness and foolishness of pride and the need for and value of true humility. You've given me some information about overcoming pride and developing more humility, but I still need more help in actually doing what the Bible says I should do. I need help putting these truths into practice." Well, how do we go about diminishing pride and developing humility in our lives? We will be answering that question in the next two chapters.

I believe that as we do this, we need to keep several things in mind. First, as we consider how to diminish sinful pride in our lives, we must be aware of what God does to humble us. God is the essential part of the process of diminishing pride in our hearts because without Him at work in us, we are powerless to change. At the same time, however, we must recognize that we ourselves have a big responsibility in this process as well. God commands us to humble ourselves under His hand (1 Peter 5:6). This command speaks to us about our part in overcoming this sin.

A third thing we need to keep in mind as we seek to diminish our pride and increase our humility quotient is the fact that there will never come a time in our lives, as long as we are in this world, when we can relax and think that we have completely conquered our propensity to be proud. The biblical commands instructing us to humble ourselves are in the present tense, meaning that obeying them is an ongoing process from which we can never take a vacation. Since the fall of man in Genesis 3, pride is as natural and common to us as breathing, whereas humility is a supernatural and uncommon virtue.

The following fictitious story of what happened to a certain man illustrates the point I'm trying to make: A certain man was given a pin by his church for being the most humble man in the church. Well, the following Sunday he proudly wore his humble pin to church to remind everyone of how humble he was. He was so proud of his humility that he wanted to display it openly to others. As a result, the church rightly decided to take his pin away from him. The point of the story? Humility is like this. As soon as we think we are humble, we're not; as soon as we think we have it, we've lost it. Like the proverbial bad penny, it keeps showing up.

Overcoming pride and increasing humility is a lifelong process. In conquering our pride, we will be involved in a battle from which we will never be entirely freed until, in the words of Scripture, "this mortal must put on immortality" (1 Cor. 15:53); until we are in the immediate presence of God in heaven where there will be no more sinful propensities in us or around us. Until then, we must fight the good fight; we must regularly exercise ourselves for the purpose of godliness.

In this chapter, we will focus on the Godward aspect of diminishing pride and increasing humility: what God uses in our lives to teach us humility. God has many means by which He gives us opportunity for growth in this crucial area of our Christian walk. It is vital that we learn to recognize these opportunities and allow God to be at work in our hearts rather than allowing these circumstances to lead us into anxiety or discontentment.

DEVELOPING TRUE HUMILITY: THE FOUNDATION

The path to true humility begins with the new birth. The Bible makes it clear that no unsaved person can be truly humble. In fact, it should not surprise us at all when unsaved people act in proud ways. Pride is the nature of the unbeliever, who does not know how to be anything else. In Psalm 10:4, the Bible describes the unbeliever like this: "The wicked, in the haughtiness of his countenance, does not seek Him. All his thoughts are, 'There is no God.' " But before we think of ourselves more highly than we ought, we must remember that we also, prior to salvation, had sinful, proud hearts. We were just as haughty and just as blind to our need for Christ as any unsaved person is by nature.

The beginning of true humility, then, is the awareness of our total depravity that comes with the initial work of the Holy Spirit in salvation. Only through the work of the Spirit in our hearts are we able to see our desperate need for God. Once we have cast ourselves on God, truly repenting of our sins and placing our faith in Him alone for forgiveness, we have begun the process of decreasing pride in our lives and increasing humility. True humility starts with the prayer of the publican: "God, be merciful to me, the sinner!" (Luke 18:13).

The second foundational means of developing true humility that God uses is the Holy Spirit. The Scripture teaches that true humility is a work of the Holy Spirit. Galatians 5:19–21 describes the things that are produced by our flesh: immorality, impurity, idolatry, strife, envy, and other evils. Most of these evils are direct manifestations of pride. According to the Word of God, we can do nothing good on our own.

The fruit of the Spirit, however, is "love, joy, peace, patience, kindness, goodness, faithfulness, gentleness, self-control..." (Gal. 5:22–23). All of these godly traits are manifestations of true humility. Proud people lack love for others, joy in all situations, peace in their relationships with other people, and patience for difficulties. Only humble people consistently exhibit the characteristics listed in Galatians 5:22–23 because these traits are produced by the Holy Spirit at work in the life of a believer. It is important, therefore, that we pray for the help and power of the Holy Spirit to produce in us the quality of humility.

Third, God uses His Word to produce humility in us. 2 Timothy 3:16 teaches, "All Scripture is inspired by God and profitable for teaching, for reproof, for correction, for training in righteousness." As we read and study the Scripture, we should be constantly reproved and corrected as the Holy Spirit shows us our sin and shows us how to overcome it.

Nehemiah relates how this happened in the life of the nation of Israel:

> Ezra opened the book in the sight of all the people for he was standing above all the people; and when he opened it, all the people stood up. Then Ezra blessed the LORD the great God. And all the people answered, "Amen, Amen!" while lifting up their hands; then they bowed low and worshiped the LORD with their faces to the ground. Also Jeshua, Bani, . . . the Levites, explained the law to the people while the people remained in their place. They read from the book, from the law of God, translating to give the sense so that they understood the reading.
>
> Then Nehemiah, who was the governor, and Ezra the priest and scribe, and the Levites who taught the people said to all the people, "This day is holy to the LORD your God; do not mourn or weep." For all the people were weeping when they heard the words of the law. (Neh. 8:5–9)

The Israelites were weeping because they had been convicted and humbled by the Word of God. They had realized how far short they fell from its standard and how in debt to God they were because of the things that they had done and not done.

Earlier, we looked at the humility of King Josiah in 2 Kings 22–23. After many years of neglect of the book of the covenant and many years of disobedience and great sinfulness among the people, the Scripture was found and read before the king and all the people. King Josiah was so overcome with sorrow for his sin and the sin of the people that he tore his robes. Then he ordered the priest Hilkiah and some others to inquire of the Lord for him.

Josiah manifested true humility by his desire to learn more about God's Word so that he and his people might walk in obedience. He realized that " 'great is the wrath of the LORD that burns against us, because our fathers have not listened to the words of this book, to do according to all that is written concerning us' " (2 Kings 22:13). The people had not listened because they and their leaders were proud.

The Lord heard Josiah's humble prayer and spared him from the destruction that was coming on the people of Israel: " 'Because your heart was tender and you humbled yourself before God when you heard His words against this place and against its inhabitants, and because you humbled yourself before Me, tore your clothes and wept before Me, I truly have heard you,' declares the LORD" (2 Chron. 34:27). Our response to the Word of God as we read it, study it, and hear it preached should be as humble as Josiah's response was. The Scripture should constantly bring us to our knees in repentance and humility as we see how sinful we are and as we realize how we have failed to take God and His commands seriously.

It follows, then, that if we wish to avail ourselves of the opportunity for reproof and correction from the Scripture, we must be willing to put ourselves under the teaching and preaching of the Word as often as possible. We must also come to the preaching and teaching of the Word with a strong desire to be shown where we are wrong and what we must do to get right. And we must be diligent to study the Word of God on our own with hearts daily seeking correction and instruction.

DEVELOPING TRUE HUMILITY:
THE REFINING FIRE

God has several other means of teaching us humility beyond the foundational aspects of saving faith, the work of the Spirit, and the reproof of His Word. These additional means could be considered part of the refining fire of difficulties that God uses to test and prove us: " 'Behold, I have refined you, but not as silver; I have tested you in the furnace of affliction' " (Isa. 48:10).

First, *God uses hard experiences to humble us.* One of the Lord's primary ways of humbling us is to put us in situations that are completely beyond our control. The Israelites experienced forty hard years in the wilderness as God taught them humility, as Moses reminded the people:

> "You shall remember all the way which the LORD your God has led you in the wilderness these forty years, that He might humble you, testing you, to know what was in your heart, whether you would keep His commandments or not. He humbled you and let you be hungry, and fed you with manna which you did not know, nor did your fathers know, that He might make you understand that man does not live by bread alone, but man lives by everything that proceeds out of the mouth of the LORD. Your clothing did not wear out on you, nor did your foot swell these forty years. Thus you are to know in your heart that the LORD your God was disciplining you just as a man disciplines his son." (Deut. 8:2–5)

God led His people into the wilderness to test them. The land where they wandered for forty years was nothing but desert wasteland. The children of Israel depended on God daily for their needs. For example, instead of providing them with a bountiful and varied diet, He chose to let them go hungry at times and to give them only manna day by day. Why did God put them through such a long time of difficulty? The Scripture says that the Lord was finding out what was in their hearts: obedience or rebellion, humility or pride.

Likewise, the Lord puts us in the wilderness at times to show us what is in our hearts. These times of testing show us our tendency toward discontentment, selfishness, and bitterness when things do not go as we wish. Ultimately, our pride is revealed as we find ourselves thinking, "I don't deserve this! Why is this happening to me?!" When the Lord's manna is not good enough for us, we may be sure that there is pride in our hearts.

God uses difficult times in our lives to teach us that there is only one reason that anything works in our lives: God ordains that it should work. The only reason things happen as they do is that He ordains them. That is what Deuteronomy 8:3 means by: "Man lives by everything that proceeds out of the mouth of the LORD." *Whatever* God ordains to be will be, and *only* what He ordains to be will be. Difficult circumstances show us the reality of our lives: we are dependent on God for *absolutely everything*!

True humility requires an absolute awareness and acknowledgment that we are utterly dependent on God. We cannot depend on anything in this world, whether it is money, a job, the food that we eat, our family, or anything else. All of these things can be taken away in an instant, as the life of Job testifies. And experiences like that of Job are sometimes what God needs to use in order to get our attention and teach us our complete dependence on Him. Praise God that He cares so much about us that He is willing to use difficult situations to show us our pride!

Second, *God uses other godly people who are wiser, more mature, more gifted, and more effective than we are to humble us.* Sometimes, when we are surrounded by people who are more gifted than we are, we become envious of them. Instead of thanking God for the gifts that we have and praising Him for the gifts of others, we wish that we had what they had. We compare our accomplishments with other people's accomplishments instead of acknowledging, "I really am nothing, and anything that God accomplishes through me is by His power."

At times, the people that God uses to humble us are scriptural examples. We might read the story of Joseph, who was mistreated by his brothers, sold into slavery, and falsely accused and thrown into jail. Joseph never became bitter or resentful of those who mistreated him, and he never complained against God because of his circumstances. Why was he able to remain obedient through many years of difficulties? Joseph did so because he was a humble man.

When we read about the life of a man such as Joseph, we should ask ourselves, "How would I respond to such difficulties? What would I do if my family mistreated me? What would I do if I were falsely accused and sent to jail?" When we compare our responses in similar circumstances to the response of a man such as Joseph, we ought to be convicted of our pride in the face of his true humility.

We may also allow ourselves to be humbled by the lives of faithful believers down through history. Recently, I have been tremendously challenged by biographies of two giants of the faith. One was a biography of William Carey, who was a missionary to India for many years. For a long time he labored for Christ with no real results, and yet he continued on in his ministry. People who should have supported his ministry financially and with prayer instead became very critical of him. He lost his first wife, married again, and struggled with rebellious children. In situation after situation, Carey experienced difficulties that would cause most of us to complain, be bitter, or throw in the towel completely.

As I read his story, I found myself thinking, "What would I have done in these situations?" Throughout his life, Carey responded with Romans 8:28, "And we know that God causes all things to work together for good to those who love God, to those who are called according to His purpose." Carey's life of humility is a helpful rebuke and challenge to me as I strive to decrease pride and increase humility in my own life.

Another was a biography of Jonathan Edwards, one of the most brilliant, learned, and gifted men America has ever known. We know him as the man who preached the message "Sinners in the Hands of an Angry God" when a large group of people were brought under conviction and professed faith in Christ. We know him as the man whom God used in an unusual way during the Great Awakening of the eighteenth century. We know him as the man who wrote numerous theological and practical books that are still being printed and studied today. We know him as the man who was the father and patriarch of a line of numerous descendants who have made significant contributions to the church and to our nation for centuries. (Among his descendants are hundreds of people who became pastors and missionaries, college presidents, government officials, college professors, etc.)

Yes, we know many of these outstanding accomplishments of Jonathan Edwards, but we don't know nearly as much about the fact that for many years Edwards was the subject of nasty, vicious, and unwarranted criticism, opposition, false rumors, and slander. What we don't know or think about nearly as much is the fact that he was hated intensely by many who did everything they could to destroy him and his family. What we don't know is the way he was mistreated in the city and church in which this gifted, competent, dedicated, humble man labored and ministered. We are often not aware of the fact that after many years of sacrificial service to the church in Northampton, Massachusetts, he was voted out of the church and asked to leave. The truth is that after many years of faithful service, the people rejected him and indicated that he and his ministry were not acceptable to them anymore. In fact, it would seem that many in the church and town hadn't liked him for most of the time he was there.

What we don't know is that Edwards did not respond in kind to his enemies; what we don't know is the way he continued to show compassion and kindness to those who reviled him and said all manner of evil against him. What we don't know about is his exemplary humility, which was as remarkable as his brilliance and giftedness. The biography of Jonathan Edwards has been a tremendous challenge to me in that it has caused me to recognize how much I lack the kind of humility that he demonstrated. It has caused me to confess my sin and to seek God's help to become more like Edwards, who was so much like his Savior.

God has used the lives of Carey and Edwards to show me my pride and (I hope) teach me some humility. And God can use the lives and struggles of many other believers for the same purpose in the lives of all of us. Oh, what lessons on humility God could teach us by studying the lives of John Bunyan, John Paton, Charles Simeon, Amy Carmichael, Joni Eareckson Tada, and countless others! Their lives are a testimony to God's grace in humbling those He loves. They should be an encouragement and challenge to us as we face difficulties, or even as we enjoy the blessing of few difficulties.

Third, *God produces humility in us by allowing other people to rebuke and criticize us.* Few things in life help us to understand the depth of our pride like our natural response to an honest rebuke or criticism. Even more so, our pride is revealed when we are criticized unjustly. The proud heart quickly rises to defend itself while the humble heart accepts the offense. God allows both just and unjust criticism to enter our lives so that we might learn humility.

In 2 Corinthians 12, we learn about the thorn in the flesh that Paul had during his ministry. Paul asked the Lord to take the thorn away, but God's response to Paul was " 'My grace is sufficient for you, for power is perfected in weakness' " (12:9). The Lord used this thorn to keep Paul humble and to cause him to depend only on Him for his needs.

Verse 10 indicates that at least part of Paul's thorn was insults and persecutions. In other words, people were going around slandering Paul and his message. In Philippians 1, we find out that some of these people were even Paul's Christian brethren. But although God could easily have caused this difficulty to be taken away, He allowed it for Paul's good. God kept Paul humble so that His power could work through Paul's weakness. Ultimately, we may be sure that Paul's ministry was more effective because of this difficulty. Had that not been the case, God could have and would have removed it.

I was recently in the state of Texas for a weekend of ministry. On Saturday evening and Sunday afternoon, my wife and I spent some time with the pastor and wife of the church where I was preaching on Sunday. As we interacted with this pastor, we both became aware of the fact that he was extremely intelligent and knowledgeable and very well educated (not because he tried to impress us, but because of the way he expressed himself and answered our questions). But along with that, we were impressed by several other character qualities that we observed in him: his compassion, his kindness, his devotion, his dedication, his servant spirit, and especially his humility. He was not hesitant to acknowledge that he had made mistakes and that he had a lot to learn. He told us that though he had been well trained in how to exegete and explain Scripture, he was woefully lacking in his ability to apply it and make it practical and relevant.

He then told us about an incident that had occurred between him and one of his fellow elders. One day the elder told him that he was leaving the church. When asked for a reason, the man said, "Because I can't understand your preaching. I just don't get it when you're preaching." The pastor asked, "What is it about my preaching you don't understand, that you don't get? Help me to know how I can make it more understandable and helpful." The pastor knew that if this man and his wife couldn't understand, there were probably others who didn't understand him, but were not brave enough to tell him. Then he had an idea about how he could use this incident to grow as a pastor. So he said to the man, "Perhaps you can help me to be a better preacher. How about our getting together for some discussion after I have prepared my message? At that time, you could look over my notes and tell me what it is you don't understand and how I could make the message more understandable. I want to preach to be understood. You could help me to improve. Would you do that?"

What an example of humility this pastor was displaying! The elder was hitting him in one of the areas where it would hurt most pastors the most. He was telling him that he was failing in one of the areas for which he had been trained and one of the most important aspects of his ministry. Yet instead of becoming defensive, instead of becoming bitter and depressed, this pastor reached out and asked for help from the very one who was criticizing him. He did not respond with stubbornness, resentment, or self-justification. In fact, in addition to asking the elder for help, he has also asked for help and instruction from those whom he recognizes as having the ability to exegete and make practical application in their preaching.

He was able to respond this way because he knew that he was not a perfect man or perfect preacher. He knew that he had a lot of room for growth and had many things he needed to learn. He was able to respond this way, too, because he believed that God was sovereign and that God had allowed this incident to happen in his life for his good and God's glory (Rom. 8:28; James 1:2–4). Because he believed the Scriptures, he was able to see the elder as the instrument God was using for a good purpose. In the same way, we can be sure that God could and would protect us from insults if He wished to. When He does not, we know that He is allowing the insults and criticisms because He knows that we need to be humbled. If people always praised us and encouraged us, we would have a tendency to think more highly of ourselves than we should. Our pride could be fed by the esteem of others. Since God wants to increase our humility, He allows us to be knocked down by others from time to time. If we truly desire to grow in humility, we must learn to gladly accept these opportunities for growth.

Fourth, and directly related to the previous point, *God allows other people to misunderstand and misrepresent us.* In other words, sometimes God permits people to ascribe to our actions motives that are not accurate. Second Corinthians tells us that the people who were slandering Paul were accusing him of doing his ministry for several reasons—pride, recognition, and monetary gain—accusations that were completely inaccurate.

Personally, one of the things that I know I struggle with most is being misrepresented or misunderstood by others. I find it very difficult, when I know what I said or did and why I said or did it, to hear that others have misunderstood me. But God has used these situations to teach me how proud I am. We cannot expect to be able to deal with a problem that we are unaware of, and so God uses difficulties such as these to teach us the depth of our pride, to bring us to repentance, and to help us grow in humility.

Fifth, *God uses our own sin and failure to humble us.* All of us make mistakes, do embarrassing things, forget to do things that we promised to do, or generally make a mess of something. When we fail and take time to reflect on our failure in a biblical way, it should not cause us to fall into self-pity or despair. Rather, it should be a helpful reminder to us that we are indeed sinful and imperfect and in desperate need of Christ. Humble people are constantly aware of their inadequacy in all things. God uses our failure to increase our humility.

I am always impressed by David's reflection on his sin in Psalm 51. For a long time, David tried to cover up his sin and refused to deal with it. But the Lord sent the prophet Nathan to confront David; when Nathan revealed David's sin to him, David was deeply convicted by it. Sometime later he wrote Psalm 51, which is titled "A Contrite Sinner's Prayer for Pardon."

What I find most amazing about this psalm is that it was written for the choir director. In other words, David wrote this psalm to be sung in the public worship services. The king, the ruler of the people, humbled himself to such an extent that he was able to write a song for the congregation that recounted his struggle to hide his sin, his repentance, and his restoration to the Lord. We might infer from this that David knew how much he needed to be reminded, over and over again, of how he had failed the Lord. The constant reminder of this public song probably helped him to continue to walk in humility before God.

For this reason, I believe that it is good for each of us to spend some time each day reflecting on how we have failed the Lord: sins of thought, word, desire, and action. If we use the Word of God as our standard for excellence, we will undoubtedly find that we have no lack of material for reflection. I believe that if we made this a regular practice, we would find it to be a tremendous help in increasing the humility in our lives because it is usually when we start to forget how sinful and fallible we really are that our hearts become proud.

The sixth kind of difficulty that God uses to humble us is *satanic opposition*. While secondary agents may be directly responsible for difficulties that we encounter, it is Satan who is orchestrating it all. This is what Paul was referring to in 2 Corinthians 12:7 when he wrote that "there was given me a thorn in the flesh, a messenger of Satan to torment me—to keep me from exalting myself." Satan was behind the insults, persecution, and difficulties that Paul was facing in his ministry, but God was ultimately behind it all because He ordained that Satan should torment Paul for Paul's own good.

When satanic or evil things come into our lives, we need to remember that God is allowing them for His purposes. Satan would never be allowed to persecute us if God did not ordain that it should be so. Thankfully, we can be confident that God is in control even of Satan. More than that, we may be sure that God is always working for our good.

It may seem strange to say that sin and the deeds of Satan can be used for good. In some respects, this can be a difficult idea to grapple with because we know that all sin is evil and detestable in God's sight. We also know that we are responsible for the sin that we commit, and that obedience is always infinitely preferable to disobedience.

At the same time, however, we recognize that God is sovereign in all things. Though we may not understand His ways, He is able to bring glory to Himself and ultimate good into our lives even through our sin and the sin of others. Somehow, the deeds of evil and oppressive tyrants will glorify God.

The tragic consequences of our own sin will somehow bring about the sovereign will of God in our lives. For this reason, as we look at the evil in the world around us, we may be encouraged rather than disheartened by the knowledge that God is in control.

TAKING STOCK OF OUR HEARTS

In this chapter, we have focused on the Godward aspects of developing true humility in our lives. In the next, we will consider the manward aspects of pursuing the quality of true humility. As we close, consider how these means of destroying pride and developing humility are at work in your own life.

Have you confessed your sin and need for a Savior, or are you still living in rebellion against God? Do you pray continually for the Holy Spirit to increase humility in your heart, or do you try to change by the power of your own will? Do you allow God's Word to convict you of sin on a regular basis, or do you neglect the Scripture? Do you graciously accept and endure difficult circumstances, knowing that God is using them to make you more like Christ, or do you become bitter and discouraged when bad things happen to you?

Do you rise above the insults, misunderstandings, and criticisms of other people, or do you quickly jump to defend and explain yourself? Do you constantly remember your own inadequacy before God as you reflect on your daily sinfulness, or do you avoid thinking about your own sin? Do you thank God for the good that He is working through evil in the world around you, or do you become frustrated with God for allowing people to suffer?

Developing humility and destroying pride is a difficult and lifelong process. Charles Spurgeon observed:

> Pride is the maddest thing that can exist. It feeds upon its own vitals. It will take away its own life, that with its blood it may make a purple robe for its shoulders. It saps and undermines its own house, that it may build its pinnacles a little higher, and then the whole structure tumbles down. Nothing proves men so mad as pride. For this they have given up rest, and ease, and repose to find rank and power among men. For this they have dared to risk their hope of salvation, to leave the gentle yoke of Jesus, and go toiling wearily along the way of life, seeking to save themselves by their own works, and at last to stagger in the mire of despair.
>
> O man, hate pride! Flee from it; abhor it. Let it not dwell with thee. If thou wantest to have a madman in your heart, embrace pride, for you shall never find one more mad than he. You may find it in any fashion you may choose: you may see it in the beggar's rags as well as in the rich man's garment. It dwells with the rich and with the poor. A man without a shoe to his foot may be as proud as if he were riding in a chariot.
>
> Pride can be found in every rank of society, among all classes of men. Sometimes it is an Arminian, and talks about the power of the creature. Then it turns Calvinistic, and boasts of its fancied security, forgetful of the Maker who alone can keep faith alive. It may be a Church man [Roman Catholic] and wor-

ship God in splendid cathedrals. It may be a dissenter, an independent, and go to the common meeting house. It is one of the most universal things in the world. It attends all kinds of chapels and churches. Look where you will, you will see pride. It comes up with us to the house of God. It goes with us to our houses. It is found in the marketplace, and in the business place, in the streets, and everywhere. . . .

Pride will get into the Christian's heart as well as the sinners'. It will flourish under the name of self-sufficiency, teaching the Christian that he is rich and increased in goods, having need of nothing. It will tell him that he doesn't need daily grace, that past experience will do for tomorrow, that he knows enough, toils enough, prays enough. It will make him forget that he has not yet attained. It will not allow him to press forward to the things that are before, forgetting the things that are behind, but enters into his heart, and tempts the believer to set up an independent business for himself. And until the Lord brings about a spiritual bankruptcy, pride will keep him from going to God.

Pride has ten thousand shapes. It is not always that stiff and starched gentleman that you picture it. It is a vile, creepy, insinuating thing that will twist itself like a serpent into our hearts. It will talk about humility and prate about being dust and ashes. I've known men talk about their corruption most marvelously, pretending to be all humility, while at the same time they were the proudest wretches that could be found this side of the gulf of separation. Oh my friends, you cannot tell how many shapes pride will assume. Look sharp about you, or you will be deceived by it, and when you think that you are entertaining angels, you will find that you have been receiving the devil unaware.[1]

APPLICATION/DISCUSSION EXERCISES

1. Review this chapter and write down all the means that God uses to decrease pride and increase humility. Be prepared to explain them to someone else and by so doing help that person to become more like the meek and humble Lord Jesus Christ.

2. From everything that was presented in this chapter, identify the most challenging and helpful things in your estimation. Explain why these truths were meaningful and challenging to you.

3. As you review this chapter, select five of the Bible verses or passages that were most challenging or helpful to you. Or if you have trouble selecting the most challenging, just select five at random. Write them out. Tell why they would be challenging or helpful in seeking to overcome pride and develop humility.

4. Select at least one Bible verse from this chapter and work on committing it to memory.

5. Study the passages from the Old Testament and New Testament lists on pages 169–71 and identify any passages that describe how God humbled people. Examples from the Old Testament: Deuteronomy 8:1–3, 16; Isaiah 2:11; 5:15; Daniel 4:19–37.

7

MORE ON HOW

As noted in previous chapters, God abhors pride and highly values humility. His Son, our Savior and Lord, was the exemplar of humility—Jesus was meek and lowly in heart, the epitome of humility. There was not even a hint of sinful pride in Him. And God is determined to make us as His people like His Son in His perfect humanity in every respect, but especially in the area of humility. According to Paul in Philippians 2:13, God is graciously at work in us to will and to do His good pleasure.

Part of His good pleasure is to make us meek and lowly in heart just like His Son. To accomplish this good purpose, God graciously and lovingly uses the circumstances we encounter in life, the study and preaching of His Word, our own sin, and the lives of other people. God's active involvement in our valley-of-humiliation experiences is certainly the most important part of the ongoing process of putting off pride and putting on humility in the lives of His people. This fact, however, doesn't mean that we just let go and let God do it without any personal effort on our part. In fact, Scripture makes it very clear that there are things we must do to develop and sustain the kind of humility that God wants us to have. James 4:10 commands, "*Humble yourselves* in the presence of the Lord, and He will exalt you." First Peter 5:6 echoes, "Therefore *humble yourselves* under the mighty hand of God, that He may exalt you at the proper time."

In many other places in Scripture as well, God makes it clear that we are to be active in developing humble hearts. Paul wrote to the Colossians, "So, as those who have been chosen of God, holy and beloved, put on a heart of . . . humility . . ." (3:12). To the Ephesian believers he wrote, "Therefore I, the prisoner of the Lord, implore you to walk in a manner worthy of the calling with which you have been called, with all humility and gentleness, with patience, showing tolerance for one another in love" (4:1–2).

How do we go about humbling ourselves? How do we put on a heart of humility? There are many, many things that we can do as believers to obey this command and, in doing so, to increase true humility in our hearts. If we are serious about becoming more like Christ, then we must pursue these things diligently and heartily.

One, in order to humble ourselves in the presence of God, *we need to spend time thinking about God's greatness and holiness in comparison to our natural, moral, and mortal insignificance.* First Peter 5:6 says, "Therefore humble yourselves under the *mighty* hand of God. . . ." We can do this by meditating on the response of men who actually stood in the presence of God.

The Scripture tells us about the apostle John's experience on the island of Patmos. John wrote, "When I saw Him, I fell at His feet like a dead man" (Rev. 1:17). Isaiah had a similar experience. When he stood before the throne of the Almighty, he cried, " 'Woe is me, for I am ruined! Because I am a man of unclean lips, and I live among a people of unclean lips; for my eyes have seen the King, the LORD of hosts' " (Isa. 6:5).

We can also magnify God in our minds by meditating on His holiness. Habakkuk 1:13 says, "Your eyes are too pure to approve evil, and You can not look on wickedness with favor." God hates sin and cannot abide it in His presence. We, on the other hand, often delight in playing with our sin—making light of it and enjoying its empty pleasures. As we think about the difference between God's utter holiness and our utter filthiness, our hearts cannot help but be humbled.

In fact, any attribute of God—faithfulness, patience, love, forgiveness—is a rebuke to us when we compare it to our own poor attempt to imitate it. The more we enlarge God in our minds, the more we will find that our image of ourselves is diminished. If we truly desire to increase in humility, we must heed the words of David in Psalm 34:3: "O magnify the LORD with me, and let us exalt His name together."

Two, *we need to think about how much God loves the humble and hates the proud.* "Hate" is a very strong word, but the Scripture makes it clear that hate is an accurate assessment of God's opinion of pride (Prov. 8:13). In fact, the Bible teaches that pride is an *abomination* to God. "Everyone who is proud in heart is an abomination to the LORD . . ." (Prov. 16:5). Calling something an abomination is probably the strongest expression of dislike available in the English language. It follows, then, that when the Lord sees pride in us, we also become an abomination to Him.

The thought of being an abomination to our Lord and Savior ought to be a terrible thing for us as believers. The last thing we should want to do is to invoke our Lord's anger against us. For that reason, when we recognize pride in our hearts, it ought to grieve us deeply and cause us to be humbled before Him. If we truly want to please God, it is helpful for us to spend time meditating on how much He hates pride and how much He loves humility in His children.

Three, if we want to diminish pride in our lives, *we need to meditate on the way that Christ humbled Himself when He came to earth.*

> Have this attitude in yourselves which was also in Christ Jesus, who, although He existed in the form of God, did not regard equality with God a thing to be grasped, but emptied Himself, taking the form of a bond-servant, and being made in the likeness of men. Being found in appearance as a man, He humbled Himself by becoming obedient to the point of death, even death on a cross. (Phil. 2:5–8)

Christ, the second person of the Holy Trinity, through whom and for whom the universe was created, became a human creature just like us. Not only that, but He was born into a humble peasant family in Nazareth. As a child, he was obedient and submissive to the very creatures that He had made—His human parents. Though He knew infinitely more than they did, He humbly submitted Himself to their authority.

Still further, Christ laid aside the independent use of His divine attributes and became obedient to the Father. He did all things by the power of the Father, depended completely on the Father, and sought the will of the Father in all things. In John 5:30 Christ explained, " 'I can do nothing on My own initiative. As I hear, I judge; and My judgment is just, because I do not seek My own will, but the will of Him who sent Me.' "

Finally, Christ humbled Himself to the point of death. He endured persecution, abuse, cruel beatings, and a horrible death at the hands of the creatures that He had made. He was dishonored and abused for sins that He neither had committed nor could commit. And He did all of this without once opening His mouth to defend or save Himself.

Proverbs 15:33 says that "before honor comes humility." Philippians 2:9 shows Christ as the ultimate example of this as well: "For this reason also, God highly exalted Him, and bestowed on Him the name which is above every name." Though Christ was greatly dishonored on earth, God has now exalted Him to the place of highest honor.

In light of Christ's humility, how can we be proud of anything? How can we ever insist on having our own way? How can we think we are better than anyone else is? How can we ever rebel against authority? If we wish to grow in humility, then we ought to spend time meditating on the tremendous humility of our Lord Jesus Christ.

Four, to diminish pride and increase humility, *we need to think seriously on the examples of humility left by the most eminent believers who have walked this earth.* Every person whom God has wonderfully used to do His work was a humble person.

That was Paul's message to the Corinthian believers in 1 Corinthians 13. The Corinthians were loaded with spiritual gifts, but Paul warned them that they were useless to God if they were impatient, unkind, or proud:

> If I speak with the tongues of men and of angels, but do not have love, I have become a noisy gong or a clanging cymbal. If I have the gift of prophecy, and know all mysteries and all knowledge; and if I have all faith, so as to remove mountains, but do not have love, I am nothing. . . .
>
> Love is patient, love is kind and is not jealous; love does not brag and is not arrogant. (1 Cor. 13:1–4)

Joseph is a good biblical example of humility for us. Genesis 41 tells us that Pharaoh had a dream involving seven fat and seven skinny cows, and then another dream with ears of grain both fat and skinny. None of Pharaoh's magicians could interpret the dream, but Pharaoh's chief cupbearer remembered how Joseph had interpreted dreams when they were in prison together. He told Pharaoh how events had unfolded exactly according to what Joseph had predicted (Gen. 41:1–13).

Pharaoh was so impressed by this information that he sent for Joseph immediately and said to him, " 'I have heard it said about you, that when you hear a dream you can interpret it.' Joseph then answered Pharaoh, saying, 'It is not in me; God will give Pharaoh a favorable answer' " (Gen. 41:15–16). Pharaoh tried to give Joseph honor by praising his ability to interpret dreams, but Joseph responded in humility, knowing that only God, the giver of dreams, could give an interpretation.

David was a humble man who frequently turned away praise. The attitude of his heart was: "Not to us, O LORD, not to us, but to Your name give glory because of Your lovingkindness, because of Your truth" (Ps. 115:1). Likewise, Paul truly believed it when he made such statements as these: "For I am the least of the apostles" (1 Cor. 15:9), "To me, the very least of all saints" (Eph. 3:8), and "Christ Jesus came into the world to save sinners, among whom I am foremost of all" (1 Tim. 1:15). And Christ declared, " 'Whoever then humbles himself as this child, he is the greatest in the kingdom of heaven' " (Matt. 18:4).

Five, if we wish to grow in humility, *we must consider the example of humility demonstrated by the holy angels.* The angels are creatures who have capacities and abilities that we do not have and can only dimly understand. They are invisible, can move about instantly from place to place, and are without sin. The Bible indicates that there is an innumerable company of angels around us, ministering spirits who are sent to those of us who are the heirs of salvation.

These wonderful, marvelous creatures are described in the Bible. In Isaiah 6 we learn what the seraphim do when they are in the presence of the Almighty God: "Seraphim stood above Him, each having six wings: with two he covered his face, and with two he covered his feet, and with two he flew. And one called out to another and said, 'Holy, Holy, Holy, is the LORD of hosts, the whole earth is full of His glory' " (Isa. 6:2–3).

The faces and feet of these glorious creatures are covered because they recognize their unworthiness in the presence of God. They are constantly in flight because they are always ready to immediately do God's will when He bids them.

The good angels, the ones who remain in heaven with the Lord, are humble even though they have never sinned, even though they always do God's will perfectly, absolutely, and without delay, and even though they have been created as beautiful, glorious beings. They never attempt to display their glory or take credit for their work. They are never unsubmissive to God. How absurd is it for us to be any less humble than these marvelous creatures who are far above us in morality, beauty, and ability! The example of the holy angels should admonish us for our sinful and foolish pride.

Six, *we need to carefully reflect on the humility of believers who are now in heaven.* There is not one proud person in heaven—not one! Revelation 4:9–11 describes what the saints in heaven are doing:

> And when the living creatures give glory and honor and thanks to Him who sits on the throne, to Him who lives forever and ever, the twenty-four elders will fall down before Him who sits on the throne, and will worship Him who lives forever and ever, and will cast their crowns before the throne, saying,
>
>> "Worthy are You, our Lord and our God, to receive glory and honor and power; for You created all things, and because of Your will they existed, and were created."

These believers in heaven are perfect now. They no longer have evil thoughts or desires; they no longer do evil things. They are pleasing to God in every way, including in their complete humility before Him. They are continuously giving God the glory that He deserves for all things. Who are we, then, that we should be proud? Instead, we ought to consider their example of true humility and do likewise.

Seven, if we want to become more humble, *we need to think about the great imperfections and weaknesses of our faith, our character, our behavior, our motives, our duties, and our service to God.* In other words, we ought to think about how frequently and grievously we sin against God. David, who was described as a man after God's own heart, wrote in Psalm 38:4, "For my iniquities are gone over my head; as a heavy burden they weigh too much for me." David humbly contemplated and acknowledged the enormity of his sin.

The Scripture tells us why we so often fail to think properly about our daily sinfulness: "All the ways of a man are clean in his own sight, but the LORD weighs the motives" (Prov. 16:2). Most of the time, we prefer either to not think about our failures or to blame others for them. Though we sin daily, how often do we confess those sins to God? Jerry Bridges has said, "We need the gospel every day."[1] How true! We need the cleansing power of Christ's blood and righteousness in our lives daily because we sin daily.

Contemplating our daily sin should help us become more humble in several ways. First, it should cause us to want to take the log out of our own eye before we consider the speck in another's eye (Matt. 7:3). In other words, it will help us to be less judgmental, which is a sign of pride. Second, it will help us to stop making excuses for our sin. Instead of blaming our circumstances, our co-workers, our supervisors, our finances, or anything else for our failures, we will humbly admit our inability to please God on our own in any way.

Many years ago, Pastor Joseph Wright was asked to open the new session of the Kansas senate with prayer. When he got up to pray, everyone present expected to hear the obligatory, politically correct, banal generalities that we usually hear in public prayers such as this. Instead, they heard a stirring prayer that passionately called our country to repentance, righteousness, and humility before the Lord.

The response to this remarkable prayer was equally passionate. A number of legislators walked out of the senate chamber during the prayer. In the six weeks that followed, Pastor Wright's church received more than five thousand phone calls regarding the prayer. Not only that, but radio commentator Paul Harvey aired Pastor Wright's prayer in its entirety on his program and received a larger response to that one program than to any other program he had previously aired.

Pastor Wright's prayer was remarkable because it expressed so accurately the way in which our nation proudly excuses its sin today. He said:

 The Word says, "Woe to those who call evil good," but that's exactly what we've done. We've lost our spiritual equilibrium and inverted our values. We confess that we have ridiculed the absolute truth of your Word and called it pluralism. We have worshipped other gods and called it multiculturalism. We have endorsed perversion and called it an alternative lifestyle. We have exploited the poor and called it the lottery. We have neglected the needy and called it self-preservation. We have rewarded laziness and called it welfare. We have killed our unborn and called it choice. We have shot abortionists and called it justifiable. We have neglected to discipline our children and called it building self-esteem. We have abused power and called it political savvy. We have coveted our neighbor's possessions and called it ambition. We have polluted the airwaves with profanity and pornography and called it freedom of expression. We have ridiculed the time-honored values of our forefathers and called it enlightenment. Search us, O God, and know our hearts today. Try us and see if there be some wicked way in us. Cleanse us from every sin and set us free. . . .[2]

Though our nation has many positive-sounding euphemisms for its wrong choices, God would call all of them sin and most of them pride.

The Puritans had an interesting habit that we might take a lesson from today. The Puritans kept journals in which they expressed and confessed their sins. If you read the journals of men such as George Whitefield and David Brainerd, you will find that these were humble men who contemplated their sin daily. God used these men because they were humble, and in the same way, if we wish to be effective in ministry and pleasing to God, we must take time each day to think about all the ways that we have failed to do and think and say everything to the glory of God.

Eight, in order to become more humble people, *we need to think about the fact that we deserve to experience God's judgment and wrath because of our sin.* This means that we need to really believe in our hearts: "I deserve to go to hell." That is an easy enough statement to say, but it is another matter entirely to mean.

Do we really believe that we deserve nothing better than to spend eternity in a place where the fire never goes out? Do we really believe that we deserve to be in a place of utter darkness, where the worm never dies, and where our sin is constantly before us? The Scripture says that before we were saved, we "were by nature children of wrath" (Eph. 2:3). If we truly believed that, we could not be proud. How can those who recognize what they truly deserve be proud?

Nine, to decrease pride and increase humility in our lives, *we need to spend time thinking about the day of judgment.* Romans 14:10 says, "For we will all stand before the judgment seat of God." The judgment is one thing that no person will be able to avoid, however great or small he was on earth. Philippians 2:10–11 teaches that eventually, "at the name of Jesus every knee will bow, of those who are in heaven and on earth and under the earth, and that every tongue will confess that Jesus Christ is Lord, to the glory of God the Father." There will be no room for pride on the day of judgment.

In our human courts, every person has the right to defend himself whether he is guilty or innocent. Sometimes people who have committed horrible crimes get away with their sin because of a good defense, believable lies, and savvy lawyers. But Romans 3:19–20 teaches, "Now we know that whatever the Law says, it speaks to those who are under the Law, so that every mouth may be closed and all the world may become accountable to God; because by the works of the Law no flesh will be justified in His sight. . . ."

When we stand in the presence of God, none of us will be able to defend ourselves. Whatever we have gotten away with on earth we will be held to account for at the judgment.

God knows us completely, and He knows our sin completely. The Scripture tells us that God will open the books on that day and that the evidence against us—every evil thought, desire, word, and action—will be given (Rev. 20:12). Sinners who refused to repent of their sins and who lived in rebellion and pride on this earth will experience the wrath and judgment of God in the hereafter. Knowing this ought to motivate us to live more humble lives.

Ten, in order to grow in humility, *we ought to reflect on the pride of Satan and the unclean spirits (or demons)*. In Isaiah 14 and Ezekiel 28, the Scripture reveals that it was pride that brought these creatures low. Satan was cast out of heaven when he boasted, " ' "I will ascend to heaven; I will raise my throne above the stars of God, and I will sit on the mount of assembly in the recesses of the north. I will ascend above the heights of the clouds; I will make myself like the Most High" ' " (Isa. 14:13–14).

Jude 6 describes what happened to Satan and the angels who followed him: "And angels who did not keep their own domain, but abandoned their proper abode, He has kept in eternal bonds under darkness for the judgment of the great day." In other words, these angels were not willing to live under the sovereignty of God.

As a result, "God did not spare angels when they sinned, but cast them into hell and committed them to pits of darkness, reserved for judgment" (2 Peter 2:4). The point that Peter was making in this passage was this: who are we to think that we will receive any less from God for our sin? If God did not spare even the angels from judgment, why would He spare us? The fall and judgment of Satan and the angels ought to be a warning to us of the severe penalty that God has reserved for pride. At the same time, it ought to also motivate us to diligently pursue humility.

Eleven, if we wish to decrease in pride and increase in humility, *we need to remember that everything that we have or have accomplished comes from God's hand.* God has given us whatever amount of money, prestige, authority, beauty, education, or wisdom that we have. Any worthwhile accomplishment of ours is so only because of God's goodness in enabling us to accomplish it.

First Corinthians 4:7 reminds us, "For who regards you as superior? What do you have that you did not receive? And if you did receive it, why do you boast as if you had not received it?" It is tempting for us to think of ourselves as being better than someone else is because we have more ability in some area. This, of course, is pride. If we want to put this pride to death, we must constantly remind ourselves of the true source of our gifts by constantly praising and thanking the Giver.

Twelve, in order to diminish pride in our lives, *we must spend time thinking about the sad consequences of pride in other people's lives.* We can start by meditating on the examples in Scripture, several of which we have already mentioned: Haman, Nebuchadnezzar, and the Pharisees. Then we can turn our thoughts to the lives of proud people such as Adolf Hitler, Saddam Hussein, and Osama bin Laden. These men have gloried in their power and in their ability to control others and have wreaked havoc on the lives of millions of people. Pride is extremely destructive, and the lives of such men bear witness to this truth.

Thirteen, *we ought to spend time with humble people and avoid as much as possible the company of arrogant people.* We often learn by the example of others more than by what they say, and an example of true humility is a wonderful characteristic to imitate. This is an important challenge to parents and grandparents. If we desire our children to be humble, then we must model humility for them. Proverbs 13:20 says, "He who walks with wise men will be wise, but the companion of fools will suffer harm."

Fourteen, in order to grow in humility, spend time thinking about how much you dislike pride in other people. The ✳ measure of our disgust for another person's pride is an excellent measure of the amount of pride in our own hearts.

In my classes at the Master's College, I often ask my students to write a response paper at the end of the course. The purpose of this paper is to give them an opportunity to think about and write down the ways in which God's truth has rebuked, convicted, or challenged them personally. This assignment is always spelled out very clearly for the students, but occasionally I receive a paper in which a student spends most of his time critiquing the authors of the course textbooks. Rather than think about what God has done to teach and admonish him through the course, the student takes the opportunity to say what he did not like about the books he read.

I find such a paper very revealing about the student who wrote it. Not only is the student unwilling to complete the assignment as given, but he has the arrogance to criticize wise and learned men of God who have undertaken to write books for his benefit. People who are unwilling to look at themselves are proud people.

Still further, if you want to grow in humility, you ought to regularly spend some time doing the following things. Spend some time thinking about how much you admire and are drawn to humble people. Think about how enjoyable it is to spend time with a humble person. Memorize and meditate on the blessings that God promises to the humble in the Scripture. The warnings that He gives to the proud will also be a great aid to you in this endeavor. And in addition to doing these things, you will find that regularly reflecting on the manifestations of pride that we discussed in earlier chapters will be a helpful means for diminishing pride and promoting humility. Review the material in those chapters, specifically identify the manifestations that you are most prone to display, and work at overcoming them.

Pray that God the Holy Spirit would produce and sustain humility in you daily. Ultimately, only God can make a person humble. Though we are responsible to pursue godliness in our lives, we can change only by God's power in us. We must spend time in prayer every day, confessing our pride to God and earnestly pleading for greater humility.

No one achieves or sustains true humility easily or quickly. Growing in humility is part of training ourselves for godliness, and we must be devoted to disciplining ourselves for it. Humility must be practiced. Though the road may be hard and long, I encourage you, as Paul did, "Let us not lose heart in doing good, for in due time we will reap if we do not grow weary" (Gal. 6:9).

I close my suggestions on what we should do to decrease pride and increase humility in our lives with a quote from a sermon by Charles Spurgeon. I include this quote because I believe that careful reflection on the facts presented in it can be a means of producing humility in us. In his sermon, preached at Park Street Chapel in 1856, Spurgeon said that

> pride is a *groundless thing*. It standeth on the sands; or worse than that, it puts its foot on the billows which yield beneath its tread; or worse still, it stands on bubbles, which soon must burst beneath its feet. Of all things pride has the worst foothold; it has no solid rock on earth whereon to place itself. We have reasons for almost everything, but we have no reasons for pride. Pride is a thing which should be unnatural to us, for we have nothing to be proud of. What is there in man of which he should glory? Our very creation is enough to humble us; what are we but creatures of to-day? Our frailty should be sufficient to lay us low, for we shall be gone to-morrow. Our ignorance should tend to keep pride from our lips. What are we, but like the wild ass's colt which knoweth nothing? And our sins ought effectually to stop our mouths, and lay us in the dust. Of all things in the world, pride towards God, is that which hath the very least excuse; it hath neither stick nor stone whereon to build. Yet like the spider, it carrieth its own web in its bowels, and can, of itself, spin that wherewith to catch its prey. It seems to stand upon itself, for it hath nothing besides whereon it can rest. Oh! man, learn to reject pride, seeing that thou hast no reason for it; whatever thou art, thou hast nothing to make thee proud. The more thou hast, the more

thou art in debt to God; and thou shouldst not be proud of that which renders thee a debtor. Consider thine origin; look back to the hole of the pit whence thou wast digged. Consider what thou wouldst have been, even now, if it were not for Divine grace. And, consider, that thou will yet be lost in hell if grace does not hold thee up. Consider that amongst the damned, there are none that would have been more damned than thyself, if grace had not kept thee from destruction. Let this consideration humble thee, that thou hast nought whereon to ground thy pride.

Again, it is a *brainless thing* as well as a groundless thing; for it brings no profit with it. There is no wisdom in a self-exaltation. Other vices have some excuse, for men seem to gain by them; avarice, pleasure, lust, have some plea; but the man who is proud sells his soul cheaply. He opens wide the flood-gates of his heart, to let men see how deep is the flood within his soul; then suddenly it floweth out, and all is gone— and all is nothing, for one puff of empty wind, one word of sweet applause—the soul is gone, and not a drop is left. In almost every other sin, we gather up the ashes when the fire is gone; but here, what is left? The covetous man hath his shining gold, but what hath the proud man? He has less than he would have had without his pride, and is no gainer whatever. Oh! man, if thou wert as mighty as Gabriel, and had all his holiness, still thou wouldst be an arrant fool to be proud, for pride would sink thee from thine angel station to the rank of devils, and bring thee from the place where Lucifer, son of the morning, once dwelt, to take up thine abode with hideous fiends in perdition. Pride exalts its head, and seeks to honor itself; but it is of all things most despised. It sought to plant crowns upon its brow, and so it hath done, but its head was hot, and it put an ice crown there, and it melted all away. Poor pride has decked itself out finely sometimes; it hath put on its most gaudy apparel, and said to others, "how brilliant I appear!" but, ah! pride, like a harlequin, dressed in thy gay colours, thou art all the more fool for that; thou art but a gazing stock for fools less foolish than thyself. Thou hast no crown, as thou thinkest thou hast, nothing solid and real, all is empty and vain. If thou, O man, desirest shame, be proud. A monarch has waded through slaughter to a throne, and shut the gates of mercy on mankind to win a little glory; but when he has exalted himself, and has been proud, worms have devoured him, like Herod, or have devoured his empire, till it passed away, and with it his pride and glory. Pride wins no crown; men never honor it, not even the menial slaves of earth; for all men look down on the proud man, and think him less than themselves. . . .

Now, I have to speak of *the seat of pride*—the heart. The true throne of pride everywhere, is the heart of man. If, my dear friends, we desire, by God's grace, to put down pride, the only way is to begin with the heart. Now let me tell you a parable, in the form of an eastern story, which will set this truth in its proper light. A wise man in the east, called a dervish, in his wanderings, came suddenly upon a mountain, and he saw beneath his feet a smiling valley, in the midst of which there flowed a river. The sun was shining on the stream, and the water as it reflected the sunlight, looked pure and beautiful. When he descended, he found it was muddy, and the water utterly unfit for drinking. Hard by he saw a young man, in the dress of a shepherd, who was with much diligence filtering the water for his flocks. At one moment he placed some water into a pitcher, and then allowing it to stand, after it had settled, he poured the clean fluid into a cistern. Then, in another place, he would be seen turning aside the current for a little, and letting it ripple over the sand and stones, that it might be filtered, and the impurities removed. The dervish watched the young man endeavouring to fill a large cistern with clear water; and he said to him, "My son, why all this toil?—what purpose dost thou answer by it?" The young man replied, "Father, I am a shepherd; this water is so filthy that my flock will not drink of it, and, therefore, I am obliged to purify it little by little, so I collect enough in this way that they may drink, but it is hard work." So saying, he wiped the sweat from his brow, for he was exhausted with his toil. "Right well hast thou laboured," said the wise man, "but dost thou know thy toil is not well applied? With half the labour thou mightest attain a better end. I should conceive that the source of this stream must be impure and polluted; let us take a pilgrimage together and see." They then walked some miles, climbing their way over many a rock, until they came to a spot where the stream took its rise. When they came near to it, they saw flocks of wild fowls flying away, and wild beasts of the earth rushing into the forest; these had come to drink, and had soiled the water with their feet. They found an open well, which kept continually flowing, but by reason of these creatures, which perpetually disturbed it, the stream was always turbid and muddy. "My son," said the wise man, "set to work now to protect the fountain and guard the well, which is the source of this stream; and when thou hast done that, if thou canst keep these wild beasts and fowls away, the stream will flow of itself, all pure and clear, and thou wilt have no longer need for thy toil." The young man did it, and as he labored, the wise man said to him, "My son, hear the word of wisdom; if thou art wrong, seek not to correct thine outward life, but seek first to get thy heart correct, for out of it are the issues of life, and thy life shall be pure when once thy heart is so." So if we would get rid of pride, we should not proceed to arrange our dress by adopting some special costume, or to qualify our language, by using an outlandish tongue, but let us seek of God that he would purify our hearts from pride, and then assuredly if pride is purged from the heart, our life also shall be humble. Make the tree good, and then the fruit shall be good; make the fountain pure, and the stream shall be sweet. Oh! that God might grant us all, by his grace, that our hearts may be kept with diligence, so that pride may never enter there lest we be haughty in our hearts, and find that afterwards cometh wrath.[3]

In typical Spurgeonic fashion, this prince of preachers has vividly and biblically exposed the nature and source of our pride problem and pointed the way to its solution.

This statement is a challenging and fitting conclusion to this book on pride and humility. Search the Scriptures to see if the truths contained in this book are so (Acts 17:11). Ponder these truths and then respond appropriately to them. Pray that God will wonderfully use the truths taught in this book to accomplish what He wants to accomplish in us and with us. I beg you, my brothers and sisters in Christ, to take these things—God's truths—to heart and let them change your heart and life. The choice is yours. Do you want to be destroyed? "Pride goes before destruction, and a haughty spirit before stumbling" (Prov. 16:18). Do you want to be honored? "The fear of the LORD is the instruction for wisdom, and before honor comes humility" (Prov. 15:33).

APPLICATION/DISCUSSION EXERCISES

1. Review this chapter and write down all the things that we can do to decrease our pride quotient and increase our humility quotient. Be prepared to explain them to someone else and by so doing help that person to become more like the meek and humble Lord Jesus Christ.

2. From everything that was presented in this chapter, identify the most challenging and helpful things in your estimation. Explain why these truths were meaningful and challenging to you.

3. As you review this chapter, select five of the Bible verses or passages that were most challenging or helpful to you. Or if you have trouble selecting the most challenging, just select five at random. Write them out. Tell why they would be challenging or helpful in seeking to overcome pride and develop humility.

4. Select at least one Bible verse from this chapter and work on committing it to memory.

5. Review and use the following Puritan prayers, which express the attitude of a truly humble person. Believing what the authors of these prayers believed about themselves and God will also be a means of fostering the kind of humility that our God desires for all His children. After reviewing and using these prayers, write out the specific things they indicate about how and what a truly humble person thinks. Reflect on these thoughts and apply them to yourself.[4]

The first of these prayers is titled "Self-Deprecation":

> O Lord,
> My every sense, member, faculty, affection, is a snare to me,
> I can scarce open my eyes but I envy those above me, or
>   despise those below.
> I all too often covet honor and riches of the mighty,
> and am proud and unmerciful to the rags of others;

If I behold beauty it is a bait to lust, or see deformity, it stirs up loathing and disdain!

How soon do slanders, vain jests, and wanton speeches creep into my heart!

Am I attractive? What fuel for pride!

Am I deformed? What an occasion for complaining and self pity!

Am I gifted? How I lust after applause!

Am I unlearned? How I despise what I have not!

Am I in authority? How prone I am to abuse my trust, make will my law, exclude others' enjoyments, serve my own interests and policy!

Am I inferior? How much I grudge the pre-eminence of others!

Am I rich? How exalted I become!

You know that all these are snares because of my corruptions, and that my greatest snare is myself.

I bewail that my understanding is so dull,

my thoughts are so trifling, my affections are so lukewarm,

my expressions are so uninspired, my life is so unbecoming;

Yet what can you expect of dust but levity, of corruption but defilement?

Keep me ever mindful of my natural state, but let me not forget my heavenly title, or the grace that can deal with every sin.

The second of these prayers is titled "Paradoxes":

O changeless God,
Under the conviction of your Spirit I learn that
the more I do, the worse I am,
the more I know, the less I know,
the more holiness I have, the more sinful I am,
the more I love, the more there is to love.
O wretched man that I am!

O Lord, I have a wild heart, and cannot stand before you;
I am like a bird before a man.
How little I love your truth and ways! I neglect prayer,
by thinking I have prayed enough and earnestly,
by knowing you have saved my soul.
Of all hypocrites, grant that I may not be an evangelical hyp-
ocrite, who sins more safely because grace abounds,
who tells his lusts that Christ's blood ignores them, who
reasons that God cannot cast him into hell regardless of how he lives for he is saved, who loves evangelical preaching, churches, Christians, but lives an
unholy, profane life.
My mind is a bucket without a bottom, with no spiritual
understanding, too little desire for the Lord's Day,
ever learning but so often not grasping the truth, always at
the gospel-well but never holding water.
My conscience is all too often without power of decision or
resolution. My heart is all too often without affec-
tion, and full of leaks.
My memory has so little retention, so I forget easily the
lessons learned, and your truths seep away.
Give me a broken heart that yet carries home the water of
grace.

BIBLICAL PASSAGES ON
PRIDE AND HUMILITY

Exodus 18:10–11
Leviticus 26:19
Deuteronomy 8:1–3, 10–16
Judges 9:7–15
1 Samuel 2:3–5
1 Kings 20:11
2 Kings 14:9–10
2 Chronicles 7:14
2 Chronicles 12:7–12
2 Chronicles 25:18–19
2 Chronicles 32:26
2 Chronicles 33:23–25
Job 11:12
Job 12:2–3
Job 15:1–13
Job 21:5–32
Job 32:9–13
Job 37:24
Psalm 9:20

Psalm 10:2–6, 11
Psalm 12:3
Psalm 16:1–11
Psalm 31:23
Psalm 49:11
Psalm 52:7
Psalm 73:6, 8–9
Psalm 75:4–6
Psalm 101:5
Psalm 119:21, 69–70, 78
Psalm 138:6
Proverbs 3:34
Proverbs 6:16–17
Proverbs 8:13
Proverbs 10:17
Proverbs 11:2, 12
Proverbs 12:9, 15
Proverbs 13:10
Proverbs 14:21

Proverbs 15:5, 10, 25, 32–33
Proverbs 16:5, 12, 18–19
Proverbs 17:19
Proverbs 18:11–12
Proverbs 20:6
Proverbs 21:4, 24
Proverbs 22:4
Proverbs 25:14, 27
Proverbs 26:5, 12, 16
Proverbs 27:2
Proverbs 28:11–12
Proverbs 29:8, 23
Proverbs 30:12–13
Isaiah 2:11–17
Isaiah 3:16–26
Isaiah 5:8, 15
Isaiah 9:9–10
Isaiah 10:5–16
Isaiah 13:11
Isaiah 14:12–16
Isaiah 23:7, 9
Isaiah 24:4, 11
Isaiah 26:5
Isaiah 28:3
Isaiah 47:7–10
Jeremiah 9:23–24
Jeremiah 13:9, 15, 17
Jeremiah 48:7, 14–15, 29
Jeremiah 49:4, 16
Jeremiah 50:31–32
Ezekiel 16:56
Ezekiel 28:2–9, 17
Ezekiel 30:6
Ezekiel 31:10–14
Daniel 4:19–37

Daniel 11:45
Hosea 5:5
Hosea 7:10
Hosea 10:11
Obadiah 1:3–4
Micah 6:8
Nahum 3:19
Habakkuk 2:4–5, 9
Zephaniah 2:10, 15
Zephaniah 3:11
Malachi 4:1

Matthew 5:3
Matthew 12:26–27
Matthew 18:1–3
Matthew 23:6–8
Matthew 23:10–12
Mark 7:21–22
Mark 10:43–45
Mark 12:38–39
Luke 1:51–52
Luke 9:46–48
Luke 14:8–11
Luke 18:9–14
Luke 20:46
Acts 20:19
Romans 1:22–30
Romans 11:17–21, 25
Romans 12:3, 16
1 Corinthians 1:29
1 Corinthians 3:1–5, 18
1 Corinthians 4:6–8, 10
1 Corinthians 5:2, 6
1 Corinthians 8:1–2
1 Corinthians 10:12

1 Corinthians 13:4

1 Corinthians 14:36–39

2 Corinthians 10:5, 12, 18

2 Corinthians 12:7

Galatians 6:3

Ephesians 4:1–3, 17

Philippians 2:3–9

Colossians 3:12

1 Timothy 2:9

1 Timothy 3:6

1 Timothy 6:1–4, 17

2 Timothy 3:2

James 3:1–3, 14–18

James 4:1–6, 10

1 Peter 5:3, 5–6

1 John 2:16

Revelation 3:17–18

Revelation 18:7–8

NOTES

Foreword

1. Quoted in Charles Bridges, *Christian Ministry* (Edinburgh: Banner of Truth Trust, 2001), 152.

2. Quoted in John Blanchard, *More Gathered Gold* (Welwyn, Hertfordshire: Evangelical Press, 1986), 249.

3. Quoted in Donald N. MacLeod, "Ministerial Pride," *Free Church Witness* (Nov. 2000), 4.

4. *Puritan Sermons 1659-1689, Being the Morning Exercises at Cripplegate* (Wheaton, Ill.: Richard Owen Roberts, 1981), 3:378.

5. MacLeod, "Ministerial Pride," 4.

6. Ibid.

7. Quoted in Bridges, *Christian Ministry,* 153.

8. Ibid., 152.

9. *God's Plot: Puritan Spirituality in Thomas Shepard's Cambridge,* ed. Michael McGiffert (Amherst: University of Massachusetts Press, 1994), 82ff.

10. *Puritan Sermons,* 3:390.

11. *Preaching and Preachers* (Grand Rapids: Zondervan, 1972), 256.

Preface

1. Charles Spurgeon, "Fear Not," The Spurgeon Archive, www.spurgeon. org/sermons/0257.htm (accessed April 8, 2005).

2. C. S. Lewis, *Mere Christianity* (San Francisco: HarperCollins, 2000), 10.

3. Chrysostom, "Homily Concerning Lowliness of Mind; And Commentary on Philippians 1:18," http://www.ccel.org/fathers/NPNF1-09/lowly.html.

Chapter 1: The Importance of Humility

1. John Bunyan, *The Pilgrim's Progress*, trans. Cheryl Ford (Wheaton, Ill.: Tyndale, 1991), 60–61.

Chapter 2: Humility toward God

1. Charles Spurgeon, "The Scales of Judgment," The Spurgeon Archive, www.spurgeon.org/sermons/0257.htm. (accessed April 8, 2005).

2. Charles Spurgeon, "The Scales of Judgment," The Spurgeon Archive, http://www.spurgeon.org/sermons/0125.htm (accessed April 8, 2005).

3. The Committee on Christian Education, Inc., The Orthodox Presbyterian Church, *Trinity Hymnal* (Philadelphia: Great Commission Publications, 1961), number 94.

4. Ibid., number 21.

Chapter 3: Portrait of Humility toward Man

1. Chrysostom, "Homily Concerning Lowliness of Mind; And Commentary on Philippians 1:18," http://www.ccel.org/fathers/NPNF1-09/lowly.html.

2. Taken from Wayne Mack notes as quoted by Dr. Stuart Scott.

3. Thomas Watson, *The Godly Man's Picture* (Edinburgh: Banner of Truth, 1992), 84.

4. Charles Spurgeon, "Pride and Humility," The Spurgeon Archive, www.spurgeon.org/sermons/0097.htm (accessed April 8, 2005).

5. C. S. Lewis, *Mere Christianity* (San Francisco: HarperCollins, 2000), 10.

6. Jonathan Edwards, *Charity and Its Fruits* (Edinburgh: Banner of Truth, 1969), 139.

Chapter 4: Completed Portrait of Humility

1. Jonathan Edwards, "Undetected Spiritual Pride," http://www.bibleteacher.org/jedw_19.htm (accessed April 8, 2005).

2. Charles Spurgeon, "Pride and Humility," The Spurgeon Archive, www.spurgeon.org/sermons/0097.htm (accessed April 8, 2005).

3. Jonathan Edwards, *Charity and Its Fruits* (Edinburgh: Banner of Truth, 1969), 142.

4. Ibid., 142–43.

Chapter 5: The Folly of Pride

1. Charles Spurgeon, "Pride and Humility," The Spurgeon Archive, www.spurgeon.org/sermons/0097.htm (accessed April 8, 2005).

2. John Newton, *Letters of John Newton* (Carlisle, Pa.: Banner of Truth Trust, 1976), 52.

3. Jack Hughes, *Expository Preaching with Word Pictures* (Rosshire, U.K.: Christian Focus, 2001), 254.

4. John Bunyan, *Grace Abounding to the Chief of Sinners* (Auburn, Mass.: Evangelical Press, 2000), 140.

5. Charles Spurgeon, "Laid Aside, Why?," *The Sword and Trowel*, May 1876, London.

6. Jonathan Edwards, "Men Naturally Are God's Enemies," www.biblebb.com/files/edwards/enemies.htm (accessed April 8,2005).

7. Ibid.

8. Jonathan Edwards, "Undetected Spiritual Pride One Cause of Failure in Times of Great Revival," www.bibleteacher.org/jedw_19.htm (accessed April 8,2005).

Chapter 6: Yes, but How?

1. Charles Spurgeon, "Pride and Humility," The Spurgeon Archive, www.spurgeon.org/sermons/0097.htm (accessed April 8, 2005).

Chapter 7: More on How

1. Jerry Bridges, *Disciplines of Grace* (Colorado Springs: NavPress, 1994), 91.

2. Joseph Wright, as heard on the Paul Harvey radio program.

3. Charles Spurgeon, "Pride and Humility," The Spurgeon Archive, www.spurgeon.org/sermons/0097.htm (accessed April 8, 2005).

4. The following prayers are from *The Valley of the Vision*, edited by Arthur Bennett (London: Banner of Truth, 2002), 128–29, 132–33.

Index of Scripture

Wayne A. Mack (M.Div., Philadelphia Theological Seminary; D.Min., Westminster Theological Seminary) is adjunct professor of biblical counseling at The Master's College and director of Strengthening Ministries International. Mack is an executive board member of F.I.R.E. (Fellowship of Independent Reformed Evangelicals) and co-pastor of Grace Fellowship Church of the Lehigh Valley. He is a charter member and executive board member of the National Association of Nouthetic Counselors. Wayne is also a member of the board of directors of the missionary agency Publicacione Fara de Gracia. He conducts seminars and conferences around the world.

Mack has authored a number of books, including *Down, but Not Out, Reaching the Ear of God; Strengthening Your Marriage; Your Family, God's Way; A Homework Manual for Biblical Living,* vols. 1 and 2; with David Swavely, *Life in the Father's House;* and with John MacArthur, *An Introduction to Biblical Counseling.* He and his wife, Carol, have four children and thirteen grandchildren. They live in the Lehigh Valley in Pennsylvania.

About Strengthening Ministries International

Strengthening Ministries International provides training and resources to strengthen you and your church. We exist to glorify God by doing what Paul and his associates did in Acts 14:21–22. They went about preaching the gospel, making disciples, strengthening the souls of those disciples, and encouraging them to continue in the faith.

Like Paul, we are dedicated to using whatever gifts and abilities, training and experience, resources and opportunities we have to strengthen Christians and churches in their commitment to Christ and in their ministries for Christ.

Fulfilling our ministry involves conducting seminars and conferences across the United States and internationally. It includes writing and distributing books, as well as developing and distributing audio and videotapes on numerous biblical, theological, and counseling subjects.

Fulfilling our purpose also includes developing and sustaining our Web site: www.mackministries.org. There you can find fuller descriptions of the various aspects of our ministry.

Strengthening Ministries International
4067 Waterford Drive
Center Valley, PA 18034

Fax: 610-282-5533
email: strengtheningmin@aol.com